Pergamon Press Ltd., Headington Hill Hall, Oxford
4 & 5 Fitzroy Square, London W.1

Pergamon Press (Scotland) Ltd., 2 & 3 Teviot Place, Edinburgh 1

Pergamon Press Inc., 44–01 21st Street, Long Island City, New York 11101

Pergamon of Canada, Ltd., 6 Adelaide Street East, Toronto, Ontario

Pergamon Press (Aust.) Pty. Ltd., 20–22 Margaret Street,
Sydney, New South Wales

Pergamon Press S.A.R.L., 24 rue des Écoles, Paris 5ᵉ

Vieweg & Sohn GmbH, Burgplatz 1, Braunschweig

Printed in Great Britain by A. Wheaton & Co. Ltd., Exeter

EDUCATION
AND SOCIAL WORK

A Symposium by

MAURICE CRAFT, LORNA RIDGWAY, OWEN WHITNEY,
CATHERINE AVENT AND NANCY HAZEL

Edited by
F. H. PEDLEY

With appendices by
HILARY HALPIN, OLIVE KENDON
and a member of AMICI

PERGAMON PRESS

OXFORD · LONDON · EDINBURGH · NEW YORK
TORONTO · SYDNEY · PARIS · BRAUNSCHWEIG

CONTENTS

v

EDITORIAL NOTE

The Pergamon Educational Guides were introduced to provide up-to-date studies of an introductory nature on various aspects of the educational and allied fields, and the series includes books on *Examinations—from Primary School to University; The Educational System in England and Wales; Children and the Law; What Happens in School; No Child is Ineducable (Special Education); and The Earliest Years. Education and Social Work* deals with the relationship between those who are involved in the operation of our educational system and those who are concerned primarily with individual casework. There is an increasing emphasis on the importance of the link between home and school, and growing appreciation of the fact that schools are not academic islands in which study can be pursued regardless of environmental influences. It was, therefore, thought important that the series should contain one volume devoted to a study of the various aspects of this problem.

In the nature of things a book of this kind could not be written by one author alone. After a brief introductory chapter, Maurice Craft discusses the different principles on which the two disciplines are based and what are the motivating factors in education and social work. Then Lorna Ridgway considers the need for a more radical approach to the problems presented by lack of co-ordination, and suggests the establishment of a "socio-educational organization" which will actively promote the interfunctioning of schools with homes and with the local community. We then move on to a detailed discussion of the education of the individual child in the wider setting—his emotional and personal education which will fit him for life as a mature member of a more mature society (by Owen Whitney) and his education for work through a broader concept of the advisory role of a Careers Service (by Catherine Avent). Lastly there are two chapters outlining the functions of the various social workers (statutory and voluntary) with whom teachers are likely to come into contact in the course of their work. There is a brief description by Nancy Hazel of their purpose, their philosophy, their links with each other, and their pattern of training, so that there can be a clearer understanding by educationists of the background to social work and the framework within which caseworkers operate.

It is a characteristic of our democratic system that however effective the welfare state may become, there are inevitably gaps which become evident over the years and with which the well-established statutory or voluntary bodies are not equipped to deal. New needs lead to the creation of new organizations to meet specific problems; as time goes on many of these are absorbed into wider organizations or, if the need fades, come to an end, having made a significant contribution in timely fashion to a developing society. To illustrate the way in which new organizations arise we asked three individuals who have been actively connected with such bodies to give a brief account of their origin, growth and function, and we have included them in appendices to this book. It is hoped that in this way there will be demonstrated the essential fact that social work is part of a living organism, and that just as the curriculum of our schools responds (perhaps too slowly) to changing needs, so there are those who are ready to give service in a practical form when and where it is most urgently needed.

It has not been thought necessary to include here a list of the names and addresses of the various organizations involved in social work, since a comprehensive list (*Guide to the Social Services*) is already produced at regular intervals by the Family Welfare Association (296 Vauxhall Bridge Rd., London S.W. 1).

ROBERT MAXWELL

F. H. PEDLEY

INTRODUCTION

F. H. PEDLEY*

THE Newsom Report (*Half Our Future*) on the education of the average and below average child in the secondary school gave a sharp jolt to those complacent educationists who, following the traditional line of the severely traditional schoolmaster, have always maintained that school is one thing and home is another—and that only rarely, perhaps at the occasional inquest evening, shall the twain be encouraged to meet. Even on these latter occasions the process can be an unedifying one—I was once embarrassed to find myself next in the queue to a parent of a child who, the teacher insisted, was not in his class; the parent was proved triumphantly right, but the interview which followed was somewhat unproductive. An unusual event this—but it illustrates the point that even now, some years later, educationists are slow to learn that their charges cannot be expected to function on two quite different wavelengths and that, in the long run, the home is bound to win if there is a conflict. Jackson and Marsden, in their very effective and moving book *Education and the Working Class*, tore apart the heart of a northern grammar school, revealing the conflicting pressures on its children and the hostility which outmoded regulations, more suited to an era which aped the public schools, could create amongst boys anxious to do their best academically but torn by loyalties to their neighbourhood.

* F. H. Pedley is the Borough Education Officer for Keighley, Yorkshire, and was at one time the Warden of an educational settlement. He is the Chairman of the Keighley International Friendship Council, Vice-chairman of the Keighley Council of Social Service, a marriage counsellor, and a member of the Executive of the National Association of Divisional Executives for Education.

In the early days of compulsory education, and in particular after the 1902 Education Act which led to swift advances in the number of poor but able boys attending grammar schools, it would perhaps have been natural for a clash to occur between home and school—though paradoxically enough at this time the privilege was so great (and the powers of the headmaster so devastating) that the gulf was accepted without opposition. Free secondary education for all, selection on the basis of ability alone, and the consequent increase in the numbers of children from working-class homes narrowed the social gap, but (again para-doxically, but in line with the factors causing all revolutions) heightened the inherent tensions. This is surely one cause of the breakaway from the most obvious absurdities of uniform ("the school cap perched on a lofty sixth former's head"), of the revolt against the artificialities of the House system and, more recently, growing adolescent opposition to traditional organized games.

Whether this analysis is true or not, the post-war years have revealed a disturbing state of affairs existing cheek by jowl with the welfare state, whilst many of the problems facing the schools seem to be more and more intractable as children mature earlier and as society bestows more freedom on its youth. "Though there has been very considerable public action", says Dr. David Glass, "there is an interlocking network of inequalities." Dr. Glass was writing the introduction to *The Home and the School*, by Dr. J. W. B. Douglas, which traces the educational progress of a large group of children born on one particular day some 20 years ago. This report shows without any shadow of doubt that, begin-ning with obvious handicaps in the sense of a poorer physical and cultural environment, children suffer, not an amelioration, but a definite intensification of these disadvantages, so that the gap between the social classes widens in spite of all that our social services are able to do. The moral according to Newsom is that we must all be social workers now and that the process of replacing slum schools and of creating better surroundings for the "under-privileged" must be speeded up.

This prescription, as the Newsom Committee was well aware, is correct though in itself inadequate, but in so far as there is the implied emphasis on the more radical individual approach to teaching, there is here the seed of real progress. What, then, has still to be done, given the right physical conditions for learning and the sympathetic approach of the born (and trained) teacher? A study of the problem suggests that success may depend on a number of related developments; first an analysis of the casework techniques of the social worker and of the ways in which these can be woven into the group situation which faces the teacher; then the cultivation of a fruitful relationship with the neighbour-hood and especially with the parents of children attending the school; next, a deliberate attempt to co-ordinate (if not in fact to some extent amalgamate) the multiplicity of social agencies involved with any family in trouble; and, finally, a careful assessment of the emotional needs of children (particularly in the most troublesome years of adolescence) with a view to the establishment of conditions in which they can come to greater maturity and ultimately contribute to society through the work which they do and which has been chosen with the help and advice of a skilled adviser.

How can these objectives be attained? In the following chapter, Maurice Craft deals with the principles on which social work is based and with their relevance to education. The core of both is the care and respect for the individual, and the teacher is in some respects better placed to make progress in that he can observe the interrelationship between one individual and his fellows, which is so often a pointer to effective action. This is not to lose sight of the fact that the school exists also (some would say mainly) for the intellectual development of its pupils, and that the level of academic attainment falls at the peril of the school's reputation. But it is to assert that a school community which recognizes the individual child as such cannot fail in the long run to be the object of high regard. The philosophy of the social worker that the most effective influence can be brought to bear only after careful consideration of the client's needs and with his full co-operation—this is the basis of a productive relationship in both fields.

The process is eased if the staff of the school can create a feeling of confidence amongst the parents whom it serves. Dr. Derek Miller of the Tavistock Institute of Human Relations referred recently to "instances of the appalling failure of communications between home and school when the school had been unaware of serious family crises and so unable to help with disturbed behaviour on the part of the child involved". This is clearly a matter of forging closer personal links, and it involves the acceptance by the teacher of his important role outside the classroom—perhaps in visiting the homes of his children. Here we come face to face with one of the inherent difficulties involved in a rationalization of the situation; there is no doubt that many parents have themselves had unhappy memories of their school life, resulting in an inbuilt distrust of schools, if not indeed an urge to give vent, through the medium of their children, to a grievance harboured over the years. Difficult though this may be, there can surely be little doubt that the only solution is to attempt to create a closer personal relationship between teacher and parent, and in these circumstances it must be the teacher, conscious of his professional duty, who goes out of his way to seek out the parent and to make contact with him on his own ground, where neither tradition nor memory is working against him. Some furrows will be hard to plough, but from most there will be a rich harvest. This is by no means to question the value of parent–teacher associations, which can be most valuable; but the parents who need most help are rarely active members.

The need for the co-ordination of the various agencies responsible for social work is readily understood, and it is becoming increasingly recognized that there should be a closer link between teachers and social workers at the training stage. "It is astonishing and regrettable", says *The Times Educational Supplement*, "that many of us can become 'fully trained' teachers without more than cursory knowledge of the special social services in touch with youngsters. You can get by at training college without any direct experience of how probation officers work, what happens to a child under an adoption order, what child guidance clinics are trying to do, what powers and duties a child care officer really has." In their evidence to the Plowden Committee on Primary Education, the Council for Social Work Training said that there was no national pattern for ensuring easy co-operation between teachers and social workers. The Council's solution was to suggest that the social services should be so arranged within the local authority that everyone concerned would know where to seek help, in the confidence that appropriate action could be taken and that they themselves would be kept fully informed. Something of the kind is certainly needed, and this is nowhere more obvious than in the weekly charades which take place in the magistrates' and juvenile courts when cases of truancy are being considered. When the mockery and the futility of the present arrangements are at last accepted, perhaps the family councils will be able to reach to the root cause and heal the divisions which now take place.

Edward Blishen has said that "schools can no longer afford to be remote or mysterious and must cultivate a more meaningful relationship with the society in which their children live". This important point has been made already, but it is perhaps worth stressing that, in addition, the relationship which is cultivated within the school between children and staff is equally decisive. Dr. M. E. M. Herford has said (in *Education*) that "without a certain basic emotional stability between pupil and teacher, education is impossible and the process is, at best, merely one of teaching a dog tricks". Dr. Herford was advocating the establishment of a comprehensive counselling service of the kind which is discussed in much greater detail in Chapters 3 and 4 of this book. What is at stake here is the provision of a healthy environment in which children and young people can, in the words of Dr. Derek Miller, "develop as productive individuals and come to terms with themselves and with society. A more significant

measure of the effectiveness of a particular education than O-
and A-level examinations provide would be to follow up children
who have left school and see how they have managed their lives."
In a society with influential mass media, where all the barriers
of modesty and reticence on intimate matters have been swept
away, it is more and more necessary to ensure that the individual
develops his own moral code, and he cannot do this without
exercise in making decisions for himself and with all the mistakes
that this will involve. School must be a place which plays its part
in helping him to reach rational decisions, based on the morality
which is implied by choice; the repercussions of this on the classroom will no doubt be profound, but it is essential, if not indeed
urgent, that they should be faced. Certainly this will become more
and more important when the school-leaving age is raised to 16
in 1970–1.

Throughout this introduction emphasis has been laid on the
contribution which can be made to education by social work
principles and by co-operation with social workers in the tasks
to be faced. This does not mean that education has nothing to
give in return. On the contrary, the lives and example of many
teachers have inspired countless children to high (often noble)
endeavour, and the tradition of concern for children which has
led to so many badly needed reforms is something to be revered.
Even the most sophisticated educationists have never sought to
become the kind of esoteric group to which one reviewer recently
referred as "the small and highly cerebral group of contributor-
type PSWs who are able to communicate with one another but
with nobody else". Pitfalls there assuredly are in the world of social
work—not least the danger of building a false wall of professionalism around a service which is essentially a personal and a friendly
one, and of manufacturing elaborate reasons for behaviour which
can be more easily explained by reference to the obvious need of
the family or the individual within it. Moreover, teaching has, in
the main, been free from the inheritance of "slumming" which
gave the voluntary social worker such a bad reputation and

charity its unhappy overtones—characteristics which are not yet entirely eliminated from the social work scene. But both teachers and social workers have much to offer to each other, much to learn, and help to give which will be sorely needed if we are to make the best use of the resources we expend on education, on the one hand, and on the nurture of the less fortunate in our society, on the other.

CHAPTER 1

EDUCATION AND SOCIAL WORK

MAURICE CRAFT, B.Sc.(Econ.), H.Dip.Ed., Acad.Dip.Ed.

Principal Lecturer in Sociology and Head of Department,
Edge Hill College of Education, Ormskirk, Lancashire*

To SOME, teaching and social work are quite different. The purposes and techniques of each role are clearly distinct and bear little relationship to each other. But to others, teaching and social work have much in common and it is the purpose of this chapter to examine some of the obvious points of contact.

Most colleges of education have experience of that minority of students who found it difficult to choose between a career in social work or one in education; or who really wanted to study child care or probation and intend to follow this up later. There are always a few older students who have come into teaching from the personnel side of industry, occasionally even from social work. Most of this small, but from year to year fairly constant group, have been involved in voluntary work with young and old, and are often drawn into college courses in sociology, social studies or youth leadership. They interpret teaching broadly and readily accept the idea of education as a social process.

* Maurice Craft was educated at the London School of Economics, Trinity College, Dublin, and the London Institute of Education, and has taught in primary and secondary schools in London and Dublin. He was appointed to Edge Hill College of Education to establish a Department of Sociology in 1960, where he is now responsible for initial and in-service courses in sociology, social work, youth leadership, vocational guidance and the education of immigrant children; and for a Department of Education and Science research project. He is currently pursuing research into educational opportunity.

1

This is perhaps a first indication that education and social work are related. When we look at the majority of students in training and at the curriculum of the college of education we quickly see that studies in human growth and behaviour figure largely (as they do in social work training), that a growing amount of attention is being given to the systematic study of social factors in education, and that practical education increasingly includes visits to child guidance units, centres for the mentally handicapped, children's homes, and juvenile courts.

Pedagogic and academic studies retain an important place but they are by no means the sole consideration of the student teacher.

EDUCATIONAL AIMS

This leads us to consider our aims in education. Are they purely pedagogic? Is the teacher mainly concerned with conveying subject matter to attentive and obedient children in a specially equipped building, as preparation for one or another set of public examinations? Is his concern limited to what happens in the classroom, between 9 a.m. and 4 p.m., and does it end when the child leaves school at 15 or 16 or 18 years of age?

In these days, we would probably regard this simplified picture of a "school-based" teacher's role as being narrow and unrealistic. "The giving and receiving of instruction"[1] is central, in order to convey the basic skills and sensitivities which our society regards as essential to its survival. But the subject matter must be relevant and living, and the children participants in its exploration. The school we would tend to see more as a focal point in the community[2] than as merely a specially equipped building. Public examinations we might regard as a necessary device for ensuring a supply of cultivated skill in an advanced industrial society, but certainly not as the dominating aim of any enlightened school or college.*

* Nor would we necessarily regard the formal public examination as being the best measuring instrument. See for example, James Hemming, *Teach them to Live*, Longmans Green, 1957.

Again, the teacher who never looks at the social setting of the school and the home background of the child, who takes no interest in the child's evening, weekend and holiday activities, and who has no thought for the child's future place in society would not today be regarded as professionally adequate. We would, perhaps, be seeking a greater awareness of the child's emotional and social life in the more "community-based" conception of the modern teacher's role.

We now begin to see further points of contact between education and social work. Where the teacher sees his class as a group of interacting personalities, each endowed with the acquired norms and values (and sometimes neuroses) of his home, street, neighbourhood, he is perhaps seeing them more as a social worker would. He is still concerned with subject matter—the cultivation of the basic skills, environmental awareness, aesthetic and spiritual insights thought valuable by our society, the *basic socialization*—this is essentially a function of the school.

But not only is the "subject matter" seen in its full social significance (history and geography are no longer lists of coronations, battles, capes and bays), but the way in which it is taught is recognized to be fraught with profound implications for emotional growth. Do the children take part, are they given any responsibility, is noise and movement taboo? Indeed, as in the youth club, the classroom "activity" will become a means rather than an end in itself in the hands of a skilled teacher—a means to facilitate emotional growth by encouraging the shy, giving experience of co-operative activity, providing the setting for success.

The modern teacher is thus likely to be aware that much more than "subject matter" is purveyed in his classroom. Equally, the values of the school may enhance or inhibit what is learned, may aid or retard mental health. And the standards and expectations of the child's peer group, family circle, and neighbourhood may almost entirely determine his receptivity and his intellectual horizons at school.

Emotional maturity is perhaps as large a concern as intellectual development in modern education. And intellectual development would, of course, include the cultivation of attitudes of mind of value in a rapidly changing industrial society, and in a democracy.* So we are concerned with rather more than the obedient acquisition of facts. We are seeking personal adjustment, the intellectual and emotional basis of good citizenship, and a supply of skilled and creative ability.

PURPOSES IN SOCIAL WORK,
AND THE OVERLAPPING OF PERSPECTIVES

If these are some of the aims and approaches of the modern teacher, how do they compare with those of the social worker? Obviously we can see clear differences; these are after all two related but none the less specialized roles in human relations. While both are concerned with socialization, education focuses on *apprenticeship*, social work on *alleviation*.

This problem-centred definition of social work seems to be widely accepted. The Younghusband Report, for example, called social work "the process of helping people, with the aid of appropriate social services, to resolve or mitigate a wide range of personal and social problems which they are unable to meet successfully without such help".[3] These handicaps might be physical, emotional, mental, or social, and they might require preventive measures, support or treatment.

The social worker's skill includes ". . . a knowledge, both broad and deep, of community resources and an understanding of people . . .",[4] that is, the ability to administer welfare services of a fairly practical kind as well as to conduct intensive casework. Thus the social worker will seek change in either, or both, the situation or the person in order to achieve a more harmonious interaction between them, and one of his first tasks is to determine

* ". . . in a democratic society 'fitting it' means also able and ready to change it" (Ottaway, A. K. C., *Education and Society*, Routledge and Kegan Paul, 1962, p. 10).

whether a problem is ". . . inside a person or outside of him . . . whether responses are situational or neurotic, whether the client has a problem or is a problem or both . . .".[5]

The social worker pursues this "ameliorative" role in three settings, individual casework, groupwork, and community organization, and of course these are not self-contained categories. *Social caseworkers* (e.g. the psychiatric social worker, or the medical social worker, formerly known as the almoner) help individuals and families to come to terms with and if possible overcome personal difficulties. *Groupworkers* might work with people of all ages, in youth clubs, community centres, or settlements, with the purpose of giving them a constructive experience of membership in a group, in order to foster personal development and enrich the community. Social work with *communities* is a largely neglected field in Britain and aims to help people to assess local needs and to mobilize resources to meet them through such organizations as councils of social service, rural community councils, community associations or settlements.

Cormack and McDougall add two more categories—the *social reformer* (pursuit of large-scale social remedies through legislation), and the *social administrator*, a "fringe" worker who is really more of a technical specialist (e.g. housing manager, personnel manager, or health visitor) than the social caseworker, who, they claim, forms "the hard core of professional social work".[6]

We now begin to see the complexities of social work, the fundamental purpose of "alleviation" being pursued in a variety of settings and thus giving rise to a variety of sub-specialisms, many of which have characteristics derived from the adjacent disciplines. Fragmentation in social work gives rise to problems comparable to those in education where nursery, infant, junior, secondary modern/technical/grammar/comprehensive schools, and centres of further, higher or informal education generally have little idea of each other's ethos and techniques.

The social worker's knowledge of neighbouring specialisms within the field of social work is as vital as his knowledge of the work of adjacent professionals in medicine, education, industry and so on, so that the referral of clients is accurate. "Case conferences" or "co-ordinating committees" attempt to overcome this excessive specialization, and the evolution of "family councils"* or of a "family service"[7] may serve the same purpose. At the same time, as in education, it has often been observed that what the various categories of clients have in common greatly exceeds their differences and the social value of such fragmentation is doubtful.

For our immediate purposes, in examining the "overlapping perspectives" of education and social work, fragmentation is a significant point of departure. The wide range of specialisms shows at once, for example, that not all social workers deal with problems of a *crisis* variety, not all work with the unbalanced, the inadequate, the abnormal. Indeed, much work is of an undramatic, routine nature, involving work with "people with straightforward or obvious needs, who require material help . . ., some simple service, or a periodic visit . . .". This was the first of three categories of caseload suggested by the Younghusband Report (para. 562), the other two involving more complex difficulties.

And if some social work has this routine character, who will deny that the teacher, on the other hand, is surprisingly often faced by disturbed children, is frequently in a crisis situation, and often has a counselling, if not a therapeutic role?[8]

To take our comparison of perspectives further, consider, for example, the role of the youth employment officer or the housing manager. (Admittedly, these are often regarded as "fringe" specialists, but they are certainly closer to social work than to industry or estate management.) The *problem* element in the work of each of these specialists is of minor importance altogether, while in education, on the other hand, the purely academic content of some teaching appointments is minor and the therapeutic function is foremost. The Crowther Report, for example, asserted: "It is our contention that teaching is always allied to other forms of

* Initially proposed for the treatment of young offenders (Cmnd. 2742, H.M.S.O., 1965).

social work, but . . . in these specially difficult districts the teacher must be more of the social worker than in other places. Indeed with some of his pupils that role must come first."[9]

Not only are the purposes and processes of education importantly qualified by sociological and social welfare considerations as suggested throughout this chapter, but we must also not lose sight of the fact that education is usually regarded as a social service anyway, and that teachers are often listed alongside social workers and doctors, as "technically qualified specialists" who, with administrative support, staff the social services.[10]

The perspectives of education and social work overlap because neither teachers nor social workers are able to provide an efficient service without involving the *personality* of the client. While Dr. Willard Waller (in a phrase which has become a cliché) states that "the school is the meeting-point of a large number of inter-tangled social relationships"[11] involving child, school and community, Dame Eileen Younghusband writes of the importance of seeing the individual in his social context, when . . . "we, the social workers, are involved in a living network of dynamic, growing, changing relationships, in which we are . . . actors in the drama".[12]

Working with and through relationships, both teacher and social worker aim to improve the client's personal adjustment and ability to make the most of his environment. As Davies and Gibson observe, they may begin at different starting points along the spectrum of possible client behaviour, need and "normality", but . . . "to help individuals from maladjustment to greater adjustment (as is customarily attempted in social work) is not essentially at variance (either in principle or purpose) with helping individuals from normal adjustment to greater self-expression and fulfilment".[13] And *fulfilment* is a second aim shared by both education and social work; both work towards the maximum development of each individual's potentialities.

These "ameliorative" and "creative" functions seem to be sufficiently common to both education and social work to justify the phrase "overlapping perspectives". It is perhaps also worth-while comparing some basic principles, for here too there is a degree of overlap.

COMMON PRINCIPLES

Take the notion of *acceptance* as it is used in social work—acceptance of each individual as being worthy of attention and respect merely as a human being, and without regard to behaviour, appearance, religion, colour, social class or anything else. This is of course fundamental to medicine and is widely practised else-where, including the education service. Most teachers do, at very least, pay lip-service to "acceptance". But in situations perceived as threatening this is more doubtful—acceptance, for example, of a child of far greater potential ability, or acceptance of the adult capabilities, vigour and "rebellion" of adolescents. [14]

In this latter case, too few teachers are really likely to take a "non-judgmental" or "non-condemnatory" standpoint, and similarly perhaps where teachers are faced with the norms and values of working-class life. There is much accumulating evidence which suggests that teachers stand for middle-class values in a largely working-class society.* Maybe the social origins of the profession and the fact that teaching is a traditional avenue of social mobility[15] account for this to a large extent. Or it might be said that those who are drawn to teaching have successfully acquired during their own educational journey lasting attitudes to the pupil/teacher relationship.

Or does this largely middle-class teachers' viewpoint partly derive from the "apprenticeship" function of the school noted earlier, the role of *socialization* which it shares with other social institutions? Schools cultivate the characteristics thought to be necessary for the survival of a complex industrial system, and for personal success within it, e.g. order, sustained effort, competitive

---

* Manual workers comprise over two-thirds of the working population in Britain.

individualism. But these are not, of course, the only qualities worth cultivating, nor are they necessarily the most appropriate to twentieth century living.

Although it could be argued that the difference in focus between education and social work suggested in the beginning (i.e. "apprenticeship" compared with "alleviation") perhaps has implications for the principle of "acceptance", it is none the less true that acceptance in education is a matter of justice and often of sound economics. The national loss of talent through deterioration of ability or early leaving is still enormous, and class prejudice in schools* may well be a factor.

Acceptance of immigrant children is equally important. Mrs. Sheila Patterson observed in her studies in several London boroughs that "some cases were noted of teachers who understand the differences in cultural background but cannot accept them; such lack of acceptance, or disapproval, is likely to emerge in their behaviour and influence the teacher–pupil relationship".[16]

As social workers frequently point out, acceptance does not imply approval, or the abandonment of a personal code of ethics. But unless there is a warm atmosphere of positive good will, effective work with (pupil or) client is much less likely.

Closely related to acceptance is the social work principle of *self-determination*, the belief that the client must be allowed and indeed encouraged to make his own decisions. Like "acceptance", this too is equally applicable in both education and social work. The modern teacher is concerned to encourage individual curiosity and an independent critical faculty. He works on the assumption that not only is this socially desirable in a democracy where the individual voice is valued, and where we regard our

* ". . . Some students may need to examine their own social preconceptions. It cannot be assumed, for example, that teachers with the same social and economic background as the pupils they teach will automatically have more insight into their pupils' difficulties; . . . they may even have less sympathy with environmental difficulties" (Newsom Report, H.M.S.O., 1963, para. 292). See, also, discussion of teachers' attitudes by Dr. Josephine Klein in Craft, M., Raynor, J. M. and Cohen, L. (Eds.), *Linking Home and School* (1967).

social and political framework as perfectible and constantly changing, but also that far more effective learning takes place where the onus of discovery is placed upon the child—where the teacher facilitates a process of active and interested exploration rather than offers secondhand description to a passive captive audience.

The social worker is similarly required to practise restraint, to encourage the client to explore a question for himself, rather than to co-operate passively in the caseworker's search for information or to listen obediently to his prescription for success. As Professor Florence Hollis has said, self-direction is stressed,

> because we believe that the soundest growth comes from within . . . . Because . . . (man) is more satisfied with conclusions he arrives at through his own thinking even when those conclusions are painful ones. Because . . . the more he exercises his innate capacity for decision making, . . . the more that capacity will grow and the more he will be able to exercise it . . . after his association with the caseworker has ended. [17]

This might almost have been written for teachers, and Professor Hollis continues: "But for this growth from within to occur there must be freedom—freedom to think, freedom to choose, freedom from condemnation, freedom from coercion, freedom to make mistakes as well as to act wisely."

Ideally, the client determines to a large degree the nature and pace of his own therapy, and this is directly paralleled in education where, again ideally, teaching material and the teacher's approach are tailored to the needs of the individual child. "Modern casework strives to be client-centred rather than procedure-centred, just as modern progressive education aims to be student-centred rather than solely on the subject." [18]

This very brief consideration of the social work concepts of acceptance and self-determination and of their relevance to education leads us perhaps to two important conclusions; first, it underlines what has already been noted, i.e. that the teaching (and of course the casework) situation involves *relationships* first and foremost. One would venture to suggest that denial of this reality (for example, in the dry, academic atmosphere of an unenlightened grammar school) is a form of defence by the teacher, defence against emotional involvement.*

Secondly, involvement has to be faced as an important constituent of the teacher's role and rendered a valuable professional instrument by *self-awareness*, awareness of one's own needs and susceptibilities, and of one's own norms and values.

In social work it is already widely recognized that emotional involvement is necessary and is not to be avoided. The social worker–client relationship is likely to be closer than friendship because it is more disinterested;[19] to use a well-known comment on the psycho-analytic situation, it may come "to the brink of love".[20] But to retain objectivity, to avoid the use of this involvement for the fulfilment of the caseworker's needs, requires self-awareness and maturity.

There will be many indirect satisfactions which (teaching or) social work may offer, but personal use of his professional relationships, or imposition of his beliefs by the (teacher or) caseworker is not legitimate. We must recognize that "in the last resort the social worker has only one piece of equipment to work with, her own personality",[21] but as Davies and Gibson write of the "social educator" (youth leader or teacher), because he works: " . . . not through something external to himself, but through himself as a person, his training cannot be effective in his work until it has touched his own attitudes and assumptions about many areas of life as a whole".[22]

A thorough-going self-awareness is fundamental.

At a rather different, more day-to-day level there are other parallels we might draw between the techniques used in education and those used in social work. For example, just as the social

* "A necessary psychological task for the entrant into any profession that works with people is the development of adequate professional detachment", writes Miss I. E. P. Menzies. But as she goes on to discuss, if elaborated into an extensive system of defence against stress and anxiety, professional effectiveness may be seriously impaired (*The Functioning of Social Systems as a defence against anxiety*, Tavistock Publications, 1961).

worker might operate as a caseworker with individuals or as a groupworker, so the teacher works constantly with individual children and regularly with and through groups (using *both* techniques, though, rather than tending to specialize in one). There is no direct parallel in the teacher's professional role to the community organizer's function. But many teachers in fact exercise this function through personal voluntary work (because many teachers have the leaning to social work discussed earlier), or through work with community service groups which are often based on the school, or through their work in professional bodies or participation in local government.

Again, a systematic, methodical approach is clearly necessary to both fields. To be able to operate effectively in the pressured situation of intensive casework or of the average school requires organizational as well as human relations skills, and increasingly so, perhaps, as social welfare provision becomes more complex and as schools become larger and curricula more extensive. We do not know if it is true that, as Younghusband has suggested, " . . . those with the temperament, the sensitivity, the insight, the imagination and the personal concern needed for good work with individuals rarely possess also the qualities of the good administrator".[23] It seems unlikely.

At all events, whether this is true or not, elementary administrative skills are indispensable, for efficiency as well as to provide a substantial basis for reflection and research.

So, too, are adequate records. In education these often comprise a few educational and health statistics for the use of the head teacher and the Education Office only. There is obviously not the same need for a regular succession of individual reports as there is in social work. But school records need to contain a far more detailed account of the social background and the changing home circumstances of each child, contributed by class teachers from time to time and *consulted* regularly by them. Individual teachers also sometimes keep their own records of the relationships of individuals or groups of children, as do youth leaders and other social group workers, in order to sharpen up the observation of attitudes and behaviour and to detect changes and trends.

Whatever the pattern, *confidentiality*, as in social work, is a primary professional requirement. When a teaching relationship comes to involve wider personal and social implications of the sort discussed in this chapter, it follows that the confidences of individual children and the facts about home background which may come to light must be treated with great respect. As the Younghusband Committee rightly claim, no information should be sought which is not relevant to the help which might be given. "There is no right to indiscriminate history-taking or discussion of a case, which may sometimes be a polite name for vulgar curiosity" (para. 623).[24]

OVERLAPPING SPECIALISMS

We have now briefly compared some of the purposes and principles of education and social work, and we have reviewed some obviously overlapping "perspectives". We have been discussing the loose collection of professional roles collectively labelled "social work" whose central function I have suggested is "alleviation", and whose fragmentation arises out of the variety and degree of personal, family and social problems which our society now identifies. Some of these social workers provide a service (e.g. in youth employment) while others attempt to influence behaviour (e.g. probation), but most probably do both in varying proportions.

This variety of social work roles, as already suggested, has led to an inevitable overlapping of functions with neighbouring professional specialisms and a continuing debate about where social work ends and an adjacent role begins. The overlap of viewpoint between social work and education, to which this chapter is devoted, is an outstanding example of this.*

* We cannot, of course, ignore the growth of the human sciences and of social policy as major factors in this situation, for *all* professional roles have "grown towards" social work with the development of knowledge and of social concern.

Thus we find frequent references to the social work element in teaching and religion, or in the work of the general practitioner, health visitor, district nurse, nursery nurse, or home help organizer.* For their part, social workers often use reference points in neighbouring specialisms to define their own methods. We are told, for example, that the casework relationship's "nearest parallel is the relationship between doctor and patient";[25] but on the other hand: "the psychiatrist, the physician, the clergyman, the lawyer, each limits his services to a single grouping of special needs. . . . The social worker in contrast works with people whose problems arise in any area of life. . . ."[26]

His concern is with the *whole* individual and his needs, in all aspects of living, and this seems a legitimate point of distinction compared with neighbouring professions, provided we bear in mind that social workers, through referral, are also apt to bring therapy to bear upon a *specific* area in their efforts to seek a client's better all-round adjustment, and their success often depends upon the accuracy of referral and the degree of co-operation between agencies.

Adjustment remains the target. As Professor Towle comments, while parents, teachers, physicians, psychiatrists and the clergy may contribute to the making of the individual, and government bodies, social and political scientists, social and economic forces help shape the environment, the social worker will operate between the two in his pursuit of the most constructive relationship (*op. cit.*)

* Varying criteria are involved in such comparisons. For example, Rodger and Dixon place emphasis on *knowledge of welfare provision* when they write that "Many workers, such as doctors, parsons and teachers could be regarded as social workers in so far as many of them are very skilled indeed in helping people; but they are not expected (in that they are not trained) to have the thorough understanding of the social services which in theory at least is also regarded as essential to all those employed as social workers . . ." (*Portrait of Social Work*, 1960, p. 204).

Or elsewhere: "A health visitor needs to know much more about the social services and how to help people take advantage of them and how to co-operate with other social workers than do doctors, teachers, or other "social workers" in the broader sense of the term" (*op. cit.*, p. 258).

To return to the spectrum of roles within social work, we have seen that these are difficult to categorize, whether by character of provision (e.g. "concrete service" or personal therapy), or as we noted earlier by the degree to which the individual worker is "problem-oriented". The housing manager, personnel officer, or National Assistance Board officer is usually claimed to be less an expert in human relations and personal therapy than a specialist in housing, industrial relations, or welfare regulations. Most of these are probably also less concerned with alleviation of a crisis variety.

But what of the community organizer (or "neighbourhood worker"), or the youth leader, whose work in each case essentially involves relationships but yet cannot be said to be primarily concerned with the alleviation of acute distress? The youth leader is a particularly interesting case because he not only illustrates these "ameliorative" and "creative" aspects of social work which we noted earlier, but also the overlapping areas of education and social work.

He is listed as a social worker in all reference works, and his techniques derive to a large extent from social group work. In the role of peripatetic youth worker with the "unattached", or where youth work is part of his appointment as a community centre warden, he is clearly exercising a social work role. He is sometimes advised to seek a qualification in a further branch of social work* to strengthen his career prospects, and so on.

Yet with the roots of modern youth leadership apparently so firmly planted in social work, the Department of Education and Science (and many appointing authorities) recognize any trained teacher as a qualified youth leader. This may, of course, simply reflect expediency. But youth leadership options are spreading in colleges of education;† and teacher/youth leader appointments

* Or in teaching. See, for example, *Training and Employment in Social Work*, N.C.S.S., 1965, p. 11.

† They now include Chelsea College of P.E., Culham, Dartford College of P.E., Edge Hill, Kenton Lodge, Kesteven, Matlock, Mount Pleasant Liverpool, Newland Park, Portsmouth, Swansea and Westhill. Other colleges are

are beginning to proliferate,* adding to the large numbers of teachers traditionally involved in part-time youth work. The informal education of the youth group is increasingly in evidence in the secondary modern fourth year, and the wider use of these techniques is supported by the Newsom Committee in their recommendation, for example, of a longer school day, and the incorporation of extra-curricular activities into the school programme.[27]

There is obviously a considerable overlap here. Youth leadership, it seems, could be considered to be on the fringes of either education or social work.† Very much the same appears to be true of some of the marginal specializations within teaching—in special educational treatment, for example. There are over 800 special schools in Britain catering for some 70,000 children and involving nearly 6000 full-time teachers. Almost half these schools are for educationally sub-normal children, but others are for the blind and partially sighted, the deaf and partially deaf, the physically handicapped, the delicate, the maladjusted and the epileptic, and those suffering from speech defects. There are also 100 schools for children confined to hospital for long periods and involving nearly 500 teachers.

Teaching in these schools clearly shares a great deal with social work. For severely mentally handicapped children there are "training centres" under the local health authorities, and teachers in these may hold a diploma of the National Association of

contemplating youth leadership courses, and the D.E.S. letter (A.T.O. 5/65) of Sept. 1965 invites further expansion.

Dr. Leslie Button's survey (N.U.T., May 1965) is a valuable source on these courses.

* The Youth Service Association claim that one-sixth of all youth leader appointments are now of this kind, and have produced a research report on the subject (July 1965).

† We see something of this overlapping of functions in Dr. D. H. Stott's advocacy of a closer tie-up of school and youth club in the prevention of delinquency, of ". . . a new kind of educationist who is part teacher and part club leader" (In *Present Needs in our work among youth*, Charles Russell Memorial Lecture, 1957, p. 13).

Mental Health in which the emphasis is less on pedagogics than on such studies as the causes of mental defect.

Home teachers of the blind and other peripatetic teachers are also on the fringes of both education and social work, and so, too, perhaps are tutors in mental hospitals or in prisons. Teachers in approved schools, which are administered under the Home Office, are expected to hold recognized teaching qualifications and are paid according to Burnham Scales, but like housemasters (for which posts teaching is a qualification) they are often regarded as social workers.

In addition to these marginal specialists in education whose work clearly overlaps with social work, there are the thousands of teachers who are responsible for remedial work in the main-stream of state education, often with children awaiting places in schools for the maladjusted or the educationally sub-normal. There are also the many teachers responsible for careers guidance (and in some cases for "counselling"); a growing number who work largely with young immigrants; and a few "teacher/social workers", whose work is discussed below. All these are "overlapping specialisms".

We find a similar overlapping between social work and medicine, where marginal specialists include the health visitor (sometimes incidentally, with the functions of school nurse, or of tutor in home-making in girls' classes*), the occupational therapist, and the speech therapist (who often works in schools). In industry, we find a clear overlap with social work in the field of industrial welfare and personnel management, in addition to that of the Youth Employment Service. In the area of social control, we find the Probation Service and the police juvenile liaison schemes.

No doubt the list of overlapping specialisms could be extended, but it is the contention of this chapter that the conjunction of education and social work is particularly marked. Not only do

* A scheme practised in nearly all the secondary modern schools in Berkshire, for example.

B

perspectives and *principles* coincide to a large degree, but there are distinct areas of *occupational* overlap too.

THE "TEACHER/SOCIAL WORKER"

One area of occupational overlap worth examining in more detail is that of the "teacher/social worker", who is a fully qualified and competent member of the teaching profession whose duties extend beyond those of the classroom and into the neighbourhood. At Edge Hill College, the training of the teacher/social worker specifically includes the cultivation of a "special sensitivity" to social background and social problems, a "sharpened perception" of deprivation or disturbance, and a greater knowledge of the appropriate neighbourhood resources available for help where needed.

As we see it (and in the light of the experience of the few such appointments in existence), the teacher/social worker will retain a clear teaching role within the school, but his commitments will be much lighter than average, and may be biased to remedial work or (in areas with a large immigrant population) to work with non-English speaking children. In secondary schools the teacher/social worker might be responsible for careers work and possibly many other aspects of guidance and counselling, and perhaps for work with fourth year groups in a variety of community-oriented studies. His duties might also include responsibility for a detailed record-card system, or for the development of active and varied parent–teacher links where they are tenuous or non-existent.

A second aspect of the teacher/social worker's role is the specific provision for *home-visiting*, either during the day or during the evening.* Initially, this contact with parents might be where children are showing signs of out-of-the-ordinary difficulties in school, or whose family background is known or suspected to be troubled. But home-visiting would not be restricted to this group.

* Many *teacher/youth leader* posts involve spending 2–3 days a week teaching and most evenings in club work. This is precisely analogous to a teacher/social worker appointment, involving, for example, 2–3 days a week teaching and the remainder free for contact with parents and neighbourhood agencies

A third most important function of the teacher/social worker is liaison with local social welfare agencies, beginning naturally with the education welfare officer, but including neighbourhood family caseworkers, health visitors, child-care officers and the probation officer, as well as youth leaders, youth employment officers, local employers and so on. He might therefore sit in on local case-conferences where appropriate. But his social work function is *identification* and *referral*, not treatment, and he would not undertake social casework with families.*

The Younghusband Committee seem to support this approach when they write:

> We are very far from suggesting that social workers have any monopoly of helping people to achieve a better adjustment between themselves and their circumstances . . . . The restoration of or improvement in ability to function acceptably is a common endeavour of medicine, *education* and religion as well as of social work. This is also one of the reasons why *teamwork and referral* are now regarded as a necessary part of successful work in these fields (para. 634, my italics).

It therefore follows that the teacher/social worker will *complement* the existing provision for linking schools with parents and with the fabric of local social services. He will work with them not replace them. In most areas the education welfare officer (formerly the "school attendance officer") is the school's chief link with the community, and the school nurse may also have contact with local families. Elsewhere, social workers may actually be attached to schools (e.g. in Glasgow), or there may be a school "care committee" (the London system involving trained social workers and voluntary committees).†

In some areas this pattern of provision will be adequate, in

* This is our approach in the training of teacher/social workers at Edge Hill College. But one could envisage a teacher/social worker who will be a qualified teacher *and also* a qualified social worker and who may in fact be involved in therapy. This is possibly nearer to the situation anticipated in Dr. Gordon Rose's Central Lancashire research project, in which the teacher/social worker appointed acts primarily as a social worker with cases referred by teachers, but also does some teaching.

† Discussed in detail in Craft, M., Raynor, J. M., and Cohen, L. (Eds.), *Linking Home and School* (1967).

others the teacher/social worker (or "home liaison officer" as the appointment is called in one school) will fill a definite need. One would certainly not claim that this is the *only* formula.[28] The distinctive contribution of the teacher/social worker, however, will be his knowledge of the classroom situation and the ethos of the school, and his three (or more) years of training in this kind of work.

Of course, many past teachers have clearly perceived the overlapping perspectives of education and social work, and have exercised this wider interpretation of their professional role. But the evidence of social research has now given us strong indications that the teacher ought to acquire, not intuitively, or incidentally and by accident but as a central tool of his trade, a detailed knowledge of the child, his family background, the social and economic structure of the immediate locality, and of the pattern of local social services. It follows that initial and in-service courses of training should embody a planned, conscious effort to alert teachers to this further dimension of their work. Notwithstanding the steady growth of sociological teaching in colleges of education, such training is at present very rare in this country.

As I have indicated, few teacher/social worker posts actually exist at the moment, but it seems very likely that the number will grow rapidly. To begin with, the Newsom Committee in discussing the school community observed that parental co-operation and support is vital. "Many situations would be helped simply by the schools knowing more of the home circumstances and the parents knowing more of what goes on in school." And, the Report continues, "there may be a strong case for having additional members of staff who have special responsibilities for home-visiting, and who act as liaison officers with all the other medical, welfare and child care services in the district. This also implies a need for teachers whose training has included some realistic sociological studies" (para. 204).

Discussing the links between school and community, the Committee considered that "... the greatest possible liaison is desirable between the schools, the youth service, the youth employment service, and all the social and welfare services which deal with young people, extending to some joint appointments of the teacher/youth leader type, or, in difficult areas, to teacher/social worker posts" (para. 293).

Since the publication of the Newsom Report, increasing attention has been given to education in deprived areas, and to the social welfare aspects of the teacher's role. In December 1964, the D.E.S. published the first of its reports on *Education Under Social Handicap*. This discussed the views of a group of head teachers who had met to consider the educational problems of difficult social environments, and its concluding paragraph was as follows:

> The appointment of social workers based on the schools would give the greatest measure of additional help . . . . *If they were qualified teachers, so much the better*. Such people could gain the co-operation of the parents in a way that "town-based" welfare workers rarely did; they could, especially, offer reassuring help to immigrant families, worried by a succession of "official" visitors. They could thus be an *invaluable link between home and school*, could take a considerable load off the head teacher, and could unite in one person services now carried out by several welfare agencies. (My italics.)

This seems to state the case in very strong and clear-cut terms and makes a number of claims which we have not time to explore further here. A point of interest is the reference to the special problems of immigrants. These certainly illustrate the clear need to link schools with home and neighbourhood for a variety of educational and social reasons, and the D.E.S. Circular six months later,[29] and the subsequent White Paper, (Cmnd. 2739), recommend the appointment of welfare assistants whose function will include helping ". . . to forge a link between the school and the parents" (para. 7).

The D.E.S. Circular quite rightly notes that the immigrants' educational problems are ". . . but one part of a much bigger problem covering also the fields of health, welfare, employment and social relationships" (para. 18). Professor John Rex, for example, has reported the fundamental importance of housing in the integration of immigrant families in Birmingham. Attention to educational problems will achieve little without alleviation of the primary problem of residential segregation and discrimination.[30]

This perhaps brings us nearer to the heart of the matter. The teacher/social worker role, we have argued, is a clear example of the overlapping perspectives and principles of education and social work. But we might put it another way and say that the teacher/ social worker role reflects the demands of our *underlying social structure*, just as the social background of the immigrant child demands particular teaching skills and a link with the home.*

For example, the population of an advanced industrial society tends to be drawn into huge urban areas, each with its "rotting inner core" involving multiple problems of overcrowding, lack of public open space, inadequacy of road systems and of all manner of public services and welfare provision.[31] And each has associated problems of ill-health, delinquency and often unemployment.[32] Urban redevelopment, on the other hand, means the creation of new, strangely quiet and "underpopulated" (and often, in the early years, highly impersonal) new communities. Complex and long established patterns of relationships are drastically affected.[33]

A second major element in the school child's social background is the social class structure with its pattern of sub-cultures; and a third is the evolution of the modern family with its changing structure and functions. These are examples of the social realities which drastically affect the work of the teacher and make it necessary for him to acquire, as we have said, a further dimension to his perception—an awareness of sociological and of social welfare aspects.

But it is when these elements combine with others to influence the educational opportunity and the educability of children that we see most clearly the need for a teacher/social worker. It is well known that the gross inequalities in educational opportunity of

* This in no way denies the need to deal with the prejudice of the parent community if we are to offer the widest range of educational opportunity to immigrant children.

pre-1944—the inability to pay fees, for example—have been largely replaced by more subtle inequalities. These are reflected in the wastage of ability throughout the educational system, and reflected most clearly in the "early leaving" of able children at the age of 15.

The Report on *Early Leaving* (1954) and the investigations of the Crowther Committee (1959) found that ". . . the outlook and assumptions of parents and children in various walks of life"[34] as demonstrated in parental attitudes towards education, the influence of friends, and neighbourhood pressure were a major factor. But the negative impact of much of school life was also a factor, and the *clash of viewpoint between home and school* thus emerges as an important theme in educational opportunity.

Working-class families are said to be characterized by short-term goals and do not place a high value on prolonged study.* (Those who do greatly influence their children's school performance.) Schools, on the other hand, tend to represent middle-class values, as suggested earlier, and teachers may undervalue the resources of working-class children.[35] Studies also show that teachers do not always fully realize or adequately cater for the sheer lack of information about educational matters on the part of working-class parents.[36] The recent work of Bernstein illustrates the gulf between home and school for many children in terms of language.

Equality of educational opportunity is thus subject to a variety of adverse social influences ". . . due to parental attitudes, customs and traditions of different social status groups, economic conditions, the attitudes of school teachers, the social climate of schools and so on".[37] And the teacher/social worker with his home-visiting function seems to be one positive way of bridging the gap between home and school.†

* Something of an over-simplification but none the less generally valid. Detailed discussion in Klein, J., *Samples from English Cultures*, Routledge and Kegan Paul, 1965.

† But as with the education of immigrants, the long-term success of educational policies is subject to the solution of such major social problems as rehousing.

As we found with Newsom, Crowther, and the D.E.S. Reports, the educational needs of the most seriously underprivileged areas have been most fully documented. And to these Reports we might add the work of Professor J. B. Mays, Dr. John Spencer, and Miss Mary Morse who each specifically advocates the notion of a teacher/social worker.[38] *Early Leaving* also advocated better liaison between school and local welfare agencies in the problem area (para. 105).

But the teacher/social worker's role, though primarily of this *ameliorative* character—linking home and school, and the early detection of maladjustment often in the prevention of delinquency—also has its *creative* aspect. Dr. Michael Young, for example, has spoken of the need to keep parents up to date in their knowledge of the curriculum and of modern teaching techniques.[39] Clearly, there is a need for teachers to establish closer links with parents in all kinds of areas.

CONCLUSION

We have now completed a brief review of several of the salient perspectives and principles of education and social work, and we have touched on some of the social welfare aspects of the teacher's role. These are particularly marked in some marginal specializations in teaching, and in the concept of the teacher/social worker they may even predominate.

We are now left with a large number of questions mostly relating to professional specialization, its advantages and its dysfunctions, in education and in social work. One of the most interesting of these is the question of *interprofessional training*, training teachers and social workers together for part or all of their respective courses.

Some 20 years ago Professor G. D. H. Cole, deploring the training of teachers in isolation, recommended that candidates for work in the applied social sciences should follow common courses, sampling various specialisms, and choosing later to become teachers, youth leaders and organizers, and social workers of various kinds. Indeed, this seems to have been proposed as a first step to an even more comprehensive pattern of basic training for the professions.[40]

In 1959 the Younghusband Report suggested that colleges of further education offering basic training in social work, in addition to offering some common courses for *different kinds* of social work training, might eventually also provide training ". . . for a variety of occupations in the field of education, health, and social work" (para. 889).

In 1963 the Robbins Report submitted that some colleges of education might ". . . wish to broaden their scope by providing courses, with a measure of common studies, for entrants to various professions in the social services".[41] While the Newsom Report (1963) was quite specific in stating that liaison between the school and local welfare services would be easier ". . . if it were possible to provide joint training facilities for teaching and the social services including youth leadership and the youth employment service" (*op. cit.*, paras. 293–4).

Since then, a working party of University and college of education tutors and social workers has been set up* to consider interprofessional training courses. University courses have begun, involving either the admission of both teachers and social workers, and the use of techniques common to both education and social work (e.g. Leicester); or involving student teachers and social workers working together on the core courses in psychology and sociology (e.g. Sussex).

In Scotland, Jordanhill College of Education, for example, offers training for teaching, youth leadership, and several branches of social work. But in England, so far, colleges of education offer only youth leadership or social science courses as *options within* the teacher training programme.

---

* April 1964, under the chairmanship of Professor J. W. Tibble, who has contributed a paper on interprofessional training to Craft, Raynor and Cohen (Eds.), *op. cit.*

The expansion of the social services, including education, in this century reflects the need for a healthy and alert labour force in a complex and expanding economy, and reflects, too, the increased value placed upon each individual member of society. Increased specialization of function within social work and within education, and a greater emphasis on social background, have followed automatically and are legitimate and desirable. But the overlap of aims and means is now so marked that common courses of training is a logical next step. Economy of resources demands it; and the risk of our developing a range of specialisms in the applied social sciences which work and think in isolation is too great for us to ignore it.[42]

REFERENCES

1. WALLER, W., *The Sociology of Teaching*, 1932.
2. See OLSEN, E., *School and Community*, 1954; or the short essay by N. GILLETT in GIBBERD, K., *Your Teenage Children*, 1964, p. 32.
3. *Report of the Working Party on Social Workers*, 1959, para. 15. PROFESSOR H. PERLMAN offers a similar definition in *Social Casework*, 1957, p. 4.
4. YOUNGHUSBAND, E. L., in *Social Casework in G.B.*, Ed. Morris, 1955, p. 197.
5. TOWLE, C., *Generic Trends in Education for Social Work*, 1956, p. 10.
6. CORMACK, U. and McDOUGALL, K., in *Social Casework in G.B.*, *op. cit.* p. 23. See also discussion in HANCOCK, A., and WILLMOTT, P., *The Social Workers*, B.B.C., 1965, Chap 2.
7. See discussion in HASTINGS, S. and JAY, P., *The Family and the Social Services*, 1965.
8. See, for example, PALMER, F. C., *Student Guidance*, 1965.
9. CENTRAL ADVISORY COUNCIL FOR EDUCATION, *15 to 18*, 1959, para. 60.
10. For example, in C.O.I., *Social Services in Britain*, 1964.
11. *Ibid.*, p. 12.
12. YOUNGHUSBAND, E. L., *Basic Training for Casework*, 1952, p. 5. See also FERARD, M. and HUNNYBUN, N., *The Caseworker's Use of Relationships*, Tavistock, 1962, and particularly the point made by BIESTEK, F. P., in *The Casework Relationship*, Allen and Unwin, 1961, on p. 19.
13. DAVIES, B. D. and GIBSON, A., *The Social Education of the Adolescent*, Chap. 9 (to be published in 1967).
14. See discussion in DAVIES, B. D. and GIBSON, A., *op. cit.*, Chap. 3.
15. See paper by FLOUD, J. and SCOTT, W., in HALSEY, A. H., FLOUD, J. and ANDERSON, C. A. (Eds.), *Education, Economy and Society*, 1961.
16. PATTERSON, S. (Ed.), *Immigrants in London*, 1963, p. 39.
17. HOLLIS, F., *Principles and Assumptions Underlying Casework Practice*, 1955.

18. TOWLE, C., *op. cit.*, p. 6.

19. Useful discussion in IRVINE, E., "What kind of Loving?", In *New Society*, 27 August 1964.

20. Quoted in TIMMS, N., *Social Casework*, 1964, p. 17.

21. WILSON, R. A., In *Social Work*, Vol. 6, No. 4, October 1949, p. 58.

22. DAVIES, B. D. and GIBSON, A., *op. cit.*, Chap. 10. See, also, the discussion in MILSON, F. W., *Social Group Method and Christian Education*, 1963, Chap. 3; or in HAMILTON, G., *Theory and Practice of Social Casework*, Columbia University Press, 1951, p. 39–43.

23. YOUNGHUSBAND, E. L., In *Social Casework in G.B.*, *op. cit.* p. 204.

24. *Ibid.*, para. 623. For a fuller discussion of basic principles in social work see BIESTEK, F. P., *op. cit.*

25. NATIONAL INSTITUTE FOR SOCIAL WORK TRAINING, *Introduction to a Social Worker*, 1964, p. 24.

26. TOWLE, C., *op. cit.*, p. 1.

27. CENTRAL ADVISORY COUNCIL FOR EDUCATION, *Half our Future*, 1963, Chap. 6.

28. A variety of possibilities are discussed in D.E.S. Report *Education Under Social Handicap* (3), 22 June 1965. DR. W. D. WALL touches on the attachment of specialist social workers to schools in GIBBERD, K., *op. cit.*, p. 31.

29. D.E.S., *The Education of Immigrants*, 14 June 1965.

30. REX, J., "Integration: the reality", in *New Society*, 12 August 1965, p. 13–15.

31. See, for example, SELF, P., *Cities in Flood*, 1961.

32. See, for example, JONES, H., *Crime in a Changing Society*, 1965, Chap. 2.

33. See, for example, YOUNG, M. and WILLMOTT, P., *Family and Kinship in E. London*, 1957.

34. CENTRAL ADVISORY COUNCIL FOR EDUCATION, *Early Leaving*, 1954, para. 97.

35. See discussion in YOUNG, M., *Innovation and Research in Education*, 1965, Chaps. 4 and 5.

36. JACKSON, B. and MARSDEN, D., *Education and the Working Class*, 1962; and also JACKSON, B., *Streaming: an education system in miniature*, 1964, p. 88, for example.

37. OTTAWAY, A. K. C., *Education and Society*, 1962, p. 135.

38. MAYS, J. B., *Education and the Urban Child*, 1962, p. 118, for example. WILSON, R., *Difficult Housing Estates*, 1963, p. 29. MORSE, M., *The Unattached*, 1965, p. 217.

39. YOUNG, M., How can parent and teacher work together? in *New Society*, 24 September 1964, p. 22. Also discussed by WALL, W. D., *Education and Mental Health*, 1955, p. 43–4.

40. COLE, G. D. H., "The aims of education", 1942, in *Essays in Social Theory*, published by Oldbourne, 1962, 62 *et seq.* See also DAVIES, H., *Culture and the Grammar School*, Routledge, 1965, p. 140.

41. H.M.S.O., *Higher Education*, 1963, para. 313.

42. See relevant discussion in FORDER, A., *Social Casework and Administration*, Faber, 1966, p. 213–4.

CHAPTER 2

A SOCIO-EDUCATIONAL SYSTEM

Lorna Ridgway, M.B.E., L.R.A.M.

*Senior Lecturer in Education, Stockwell College of Education,
Bromley, Kent**

The full participation of the community in education would mean the emergence, both in idea and in actual organisation, of a fuller interpretation of the meaning of education, at present no more than adumbrated by the multiplicity of separate and imperfectly co-ordinated services, medical, educational, disciplinary, recreational, and so on. The absorption of education, in the narrower sense, into such a comprehensive service, and the consequent enlargement of what education means, may be far more important than any changes in the schools themselves, and may constitute the real educational revolution of our time.

Jeffreys, M. V. C., Professor of Education, University of Birmingham, and Director of the University of Birmingham Institute of Education, writing of "School and Community", in *Glaucon.*

Is our present education system fully effective?

In all honesty we must admit that it is not. The high levels of academic performance achieved by a proportion of the nation's children are more than satisfactory, but must be balanced against disappointment and anxiety concerning the school failures—the under-functioning pupils and early leavers, and against the national figures for delinquency, maladjustment, neurosis and crime.

* Mrs. L. M. Ridgway formerly taught in London schools and was for 15 years a head teacher. She is specially interested in the creative thinking of children (particularly in music), the liberalisation of school and college curricula and in the promotion of better understanding between schools and society. With I. Lawton she is the author of *Family Grouping in the Infants' School.*

The ethos and social attitudes of the community must bear their measure of responsibility, but it is clear that at some point or points along the educational continuum precious human and financial resources are being dissipated. Teachers toil to educate children who benefit only partially from their efforts. Perhaps the programmes of work are unsuitable; it may be that the children are preoccupied, at conscious or unconscious level, with other matters more pertinent to their lives. Many explanations might be given, but the fact remains that the teaching is ultimately only partially effective. Similarly, social workers labour to pick up the disintegrated or disintegrating pieces of children's lives, and doctors, psychologists, magistrates and juvenile officers add their quota of trained and dedicated effort, backed by public money, to cure, reform or restrain children whose response to their educational or social environment is inadequate or downright antagonistic.

How is this wastage of human potential, human effort and money to be arrested? And, in the words of James Hemming, "If the future of scientific society depends upon improving the personal development of its members, how may education contribute to this end?"[1]

A twofold approach is here suggested, which might lead to some improvement. On the one hand, educationists need to re-think their priorities: on the other, there is the need for closer integration between the educational, welfare and juvenile services which at present function so often in near isolation.*

It is frequently stated that the education which every child receives should be planned to develop fully his or her potential ability, firstly because of the supreme importance of the individual, and of his maximum self-realization, and secondly so that society as a whole may benefit. Since society can only progress through the achievements of its members, the cultivation of the full

* For example, writing in 1964 of the White Paper on *The Child, the Family and the Young Offender*, Barbara Wootton says, "So far as the White Paper is concerned, the whole educational system might not exist".

ability of each member leads directly to the improvement of all.

It is perhaps not so generally accepted in education that the full development of individual capacities initially depends, not upon the provision of the right "kind" of education (in the narrow traditional sense of areas of knowledge to be studied or skills cultivated), but upon the proper integration and development of personality, intellectual ability being seen as only one element in personality structure. A vitally significant part of this integrating process occurs in babyhood,[2] but intellectual progress can be stunted at any age by poverty of social experience, and it can be distorted or frustrated at any level by unsatisfactory emotional development. Evidence for this is mounting, and is freely available to teachers and to parents.[3]

Nevertheless, the former, and to some extent the latter also, only too often attempt to separate off *an* element in the school child—an educable portion of personality—which the school is to cultivate, whilst the home, church, youth club, or some other social unit deals with the rest.

Certainly the development of skills and abilities and the traditional transmission of knowledge and culture are central to the task of the school. But the task cannot be seen in isolation. If it is to be successful for each pupil, and to perform its proper function in society, the educational system must concern itself in the first instance with the emotional, social and intellectual integration of each developing child. And since neither the children nor the school itself can function satisfactorily in a social vacuum the school community must cultivate purposeful co-operative interaction with the other social groups in which a child moves.

In early childhood the most important of these is, of course, the family. But even with the supremely important nuclear family group, school contact is often only too infrequent. Parents are sometimes actively discouraged from entering the school, or from "interfering" in the education of their own children, and the idea that any parent could satisfactorily take responsibility for the education of his or her own children is regarded with incredulity.[4] In the vital cases where breakdowns in children's lives are occurring, the liaison between home and school may be deplorably indirect; with clubs and other external children's organizations there may be virtually no contact at all.* All too often a child leads a strangely fragmented life as far as the significant adults in it are concerned. Mrs. Floud[3] refers to the "assumption" that "the interaction between home and school is the key to educability"—is this assumption always acted upon?

The traditional role of education is that of concern for academic attainment. It is true that many individual teachers have a care for the social issues implicit in their educational task, and there are enlightened schools which are focal points for broader community services, but teachers on the whole do not see these issues—or contact with these activities—as their concern. Neither do many parents. A recent investigation[5] involving 470 grammar, secondary modern, junior and infant school teachers concluded that "in all types of school, teachers saw their role primarily in intellectual and moral terms, and were comparatively indifferent to more general social training". It also stated, somewhat surprisingly, that "married women junior school teachers had a more restricted view of their role than single teachers". Broadly speaking, the same views were held by the children's parents.

Teachers alone cannot alter this situation. First must come general understanding of the need for new thinking. A fresh look must be taken at the concept underlying the term "education", and at the function of the school within the community, with a shift of emphasis away from the pressure to develop intellectual powers in isolation. This for many children is self-defeating, and leads to a waste of potential ability which in some circumstances is pitiful and in others frightening.

What is the alternative to a closed school system concentrating on academic prowess? It is, I submit, a *socio-educational system*

* Closer contact between youth employment officers and schools is recommended in the Albermarle Report.

genuinely responsible for the full development of the personality structure of each child including his intellectual capacity, establishing widening social contacts, providing for the contribution of each to the group, and linking up closely with the network of social and welfare services concerned with the well-being of children.

THE FAMILY AND THE SCHOOL

The twentieth-century child is socially and emotionally impoverished in that his education no longer takes place in the more primitive family situation. D. W. Winnicott[2] refers to "a significant change in the family pattern", in that there is a "relative lack, not only of brothers and sisters, but also of cousins". Contact with related adults is also often minimal. In more primitive societies, aunts, uncles, grandparents and pseudo-relatives provide a broad stable area of affection and discipline within which social experience, at once supporting and educative, can occur. For today's child, school virtually takes the place of the extended family, and should seek to provide social and emotional nutriment as well as intellectual food.

Schools opening their doors and initiating a change of attitude have nothing to lose and everything to gain. All those with personal and intimate knowledge of any one child can come together to act in concert in his or her interests. The operative factor is *personal* knowledge. How many parents and teachers (not head teachers) spend time talking to one another? In a recent instance the mother of a disorderly 15-year-old girl was interviewed at school by the head teacher and the head of the senior school, but had no chance to talk to the girl's form teacher, the only adult in constant daily contact with the child.

Many mothers and fathers are genuinely afraid of contacting their children's schools for fear of being thought interfering or fussy. Yet it is they who must hand over their children to others for the long impressionable hours of childhood and youth. Active encouragement of their interest, as well as using "the double bonds"*[(6)] of the child to help him might also arouse militant interest, and accelerate improvement in the shocking state of schools as revealed in two recent surveys.† Mothers already help voluntarily in many schools, by acting as escorts, by sewing, supervising groups and so on; fathers teach sports and pastimes, give talks, make apparatus, garden and build swimming pools. "Why should not a father who is a scientist be released part-time from his work to teach science in his children's school, and then take the class to the laboratory where he works so that he can show the application of scientific knowledge to practical work?"‡ Only the rigidity of traditional thinking about the relative roles of teachers and parents makes such a suggestion appear unacceptable.

But there are also traditional regulations hedged around the schools, which, although making for ease of administration, allow too little of the flexibility needed for dealing with human beings. Simple relaxation of rules and traditions would, for instance, allow for adaptability in the age of entry into school. Mothers know that some children are ready at $4\frac{1}{2}$ years, while others would be better at home until they are 6 years old.§

The desirability of elasticity in the hours of attendance, particularly in the early years, is also well known. It has been frequently acknowledged, but so far virtually ignored in practice, that for some children a 5-hour school day (sometimes made longer by a school dinner-hour) is too long. Some head teachers, guided by commonsense, take responsibility upon themselves and relax the rules. Such enterprising changes in practice herald what should

* Arnold Gesell's telling phrase.

† 1962 (The Ministry of Education, The National Union of Teachers).

‡ Anthony Wedgwood Benn, M.P., writing on "Schools and People", *The Guardian*, 1965.

§ Great Britain alone of the great nations requires compulsory school attendance at 5 years. In Sweden, where academic and cultural standards are high, compulsory schooling starts at 7 years without apparent detriment to future performance.

forthwith be regularized by a change in law. Most adults are so far removed from the experiences of their early childhood years, that the variation of an hour or two or of a few months spent in the educational machine may seem of small importance. Children are very adaptable, they say, and in any case sooner or later have to face up to situations they may not like. "They get used to it" covers a multitude of unwitting offences against children. But many mothers—and some teachers—are aware that "they" do not "get used to it", or that this process is a painful one building up attitudes of fear, dislike or rejection which may adversely affect receptiveness to learning for the rest of life. Comparatively small modifications in the early stages might well reap later educational rewards, particularly in the establishment of desirable attitudes to education, as well as strengthening the bonds of understanding between home and school.

Similarly, there is little doubt that children's performance at junior and secondary school level is strongly influenced by confidence and satisfaction engendered by successful experience in the infant school years. There, traditional school organization might well give way to allow for the consistent handling and other benefits which family (vertical age) grouping promotes.* In a small community of mixed ages there is a natural social climate in which caring for others and the acceptance of responsibility—both basic ingredients of good citizenship—are daily exercised along with individual intellectual powers. Checks due to insecurity and change are avoided;[7] children and adults know each other better, and many of the hazards which impede optimum personal development can be intercepted and deflected, whilst the effects

* Traditional organization is in fact giving way. Vertically age grouped infant schools are to be found in Berkshire, Bristol, Cambridgeshire, Devon, Essex, Hertfordshire, Kent, Leicestershire, London, Middlesex, Nottingham, Oxfordshire, the West Riding of Yorkshire, in the British Forces schools in Germany, and probably in many other areas. Similar experiments are going on in junior schools.

In 1967 the I.L.E.A. expects to open a second J.M. and I. school where flexibility of planning is designed to bridge the gaps which customarily occur at transfer points between nursery, infant and junior education.

of those which are unavoidable can be anticipated and mitigated. Casualties can be prevented, rather than rescued.

After early school life should come continuous pastoral care (a forerunner of which is creeping into some secondary schools in the form of "counselling"), with the children, perhaps of mixed ages, in small stable groups around one or more adults, as is already being done in the tutorial or house systems of some public and comprehensive schools.

For such a programme the traditional role of teachers needs reviewing in the light of children's psycho-social needs. It cannot be carried out by teachers alone, but necessitates co-operation with social, welfare and psychiatric workers whose contributions would become progressively more constructive and less those of rescue and remedial work, much as preventive medicine has already virtually eliminated in this country diseases such as diphtheria and smallpox.*[8] Maladjustment and delinquency could be foreseen and perhaps prevented, rather than being left to develop until abnormal behaviour forces therapeutic measures.

By puberty, wider, purposefully constructed social contributions need to be arranged for all children, perhaps through the tutorial groups already suggested. At present such opportunities depend upon the haphazard chance of belonging to an enterprising school or youth group.[9]

The initiative of individuals points the way into the future. The pioneer work of a few brought forth the infants' school and nursery education: in more recent times the privately formed Spastics Association has led to dramatic advances in the educational treatment of handicapped children: another straw in the prevailing wind is the unofficial formation of play-groups for under-fives. Just so, a recently opened school† has been deliberately constructed as a focus for local communal activity. The swimming

* Unhappily the Pioneer Health Centre at Peckham, with its emphasis on an integrated family medical and recreational service, died for lack of financial support (see Williamson, G., Scott, Pearse, Innes, H., *Science, Synthesis and Sanity*).

† At Ollerton, Northants, a new comprehensive school incorporates a residential training centre for youth leaders and a further education and youth wing.

pool, library, sports hall and theatre are available for the use of the local community, and the sixth-form refectory provides facilities for further and adult education in the evening.

Here the educational service has taken on a totally new image, and deliberately sets out to cultivate a closer and more significant relationship with the outside world. There seems no reason why every school should not make a start along these lines, to the mutual benefit of school and local community. Teachers may, in the first instance, see this as a burdensome extension of their obligations. But, apart from the enrichment of their pupils' schooling, schools would have much to gain. Primary schools in particular, where staff shortages will become increasingly severe over the next decade, possibly even until the turn of the century,* need to survey rapidly and with clear-sighted objectivity all means open to them to relieve the pressures of over-large classes. Auxiliary help is desperately needed in primary schools, and teachers would be well advised to welcome it in whatever form it is available: it need by no means usurp their traditional roles and responsibilities. Cautious experimentation in some schools with paid and unpaid parental help in meals or play supervision, secretarial and escort duties, even in classroom ancillary aid, has shown that we are only on the fringe of what can be achieved by the furtherance of parent–teacher partnership. Hospitals have "Leagues of Friends": why not schools?†

* "There is little doubt that the next twenty years' progress in the services of education will be conditioned to a very great extent by the availability of the necessary teaching staff. The impact of the shortage of teachers will strike most severely at the primary schools and particularly at the Infant schools" (Sir William Alexander, *Education*, June 1964).

"The Ninth Report of the National Advisory Council for the Training and Supply of Teachers makes no separate study of the staffing of Infants' schools, and offers no suggestions to meet present or future shortages. The proposed changes in the balance of sexes admitted to Colleges of Education will make no contribution to the staffing of Infants' schools" (George Taylor, *Education*, December 1964).

† "The Eastwood Association", a body of teachers, parents, children, former pupils and friends of Eastwood School, Keighley, offers a useful line of development.

But an overall policy needs instituting. The level of co-operation and understanding within the educational system itself, between teacher and teacher, school and school, and particularly between one type of school and another, is often deplorably low, and the degree of purposeful effort which would be needed to throw off traditional attitudes and actively to pursue a policy of social inter-relationships is likely to be more than individual schools and teachers can undertake unaided. Teachers are for the most part fully extended and unable to respond to exhortations to do more.

AIDS FOR THE TEACHER

Along with a nationally organized policy of integrating family, school and social services needs to go a deliberate programme aimed at making better use of the time and energy of the teachers themselves, especially as their numbers, already inadequate, show no sign of expanding fast enough to keep pace with the foreseeable demand.

Research into methods of improving teaching techniques could result in more being taught in less time: a programme of research is needed into the ways in which differing children learn best (for instance, in audio or visual ways, in synthetic or analytic), and into the timing of teaching at appropriate stages of readiness. The work of Piaget* has underlined the dangers, in some areas of learning, of specific teaching undertaken too soon: Dr. Tanner hints at the lost opportunities of teaching left too late. [10] The unfortunate teacher, proceeding by rule of thumb and struggling to keep up to date with new research, needs informed guidance and proper opportunity for in-service refresher courses.

Further helpful investigation must be made into the uses of teaching machines and programmed learning. Appropriately and properly used, they can and will alter the whole character of

* See, for instance, *Some aspects of Piaget's Work*, National Froebel Foundation publication.

further, secondary and perhaps even later-stage primary education. Traditional educationalists must abandon the idea of *teaching* in a rigid class situation of 30–40 children, and envisage a flexible programme of children *learning*, sometimes in groups of 100 or more, with television or illustrated lecture, sometimes in tutorial groups of 6–12, and sometimes in the individual learning situation of the language laboratory, or by individual instruction at the teaching machine. These scientific aids are with us. Only the understanding and ability to make the best and fullest use of them lags behind. A lead is being given by some able and farsighted teachers: programmes are beginning to pour out: but commercial interests cannot be left to flood the market with ill-designed or unsuitable programmes. Teachers need skilled help and advice and that quickly.*

There would be a rapid repayment in improved quality of learning, and also in the wider choice of specializations which would automatically be made available to children in secondary and further education. Further liberalization of secondary education would be possible: streaming could give place, as it is already doing, to the more flexible setting across classes and age groups, and to a combination of group work assignments and individual study.

There is need also for a close look at the factors which govern specialization. At present genetic ability factors or those of individual interest are sometimes forced to give way to environmental opportunity. A child once launched on a path of specialized learning in secondary school, having chosen from what may be the limited possibilities available, is frequently unable to turn aside from that particular track until O- and A-levels have taken him relentlessly forward into predestined study in further education. Thus an unenlightened or enforced choice at 13+ may presage disillusionment and lack of enthusiasm in the late teens or

---

* "If television can make scarce teachers more widely available, it can only do so effectively if they know how to use the television medium" (Norman E. Willis, *Education*, January 1965).

early twenties. Some universities,* realizing the danger, have taken steps to widen the possibilities for their students. But the supplementing of teaching strengths in secondary schools and colleges by an adequate provision of automated teaching aids should make it possible to offer broader programmes of academic, cultural and practical education. Time and money will have to be spent, however, not only upon reviewing the new possibilities, but also upon teaching teachers to understand them.

These opportunities may well be extended into adult education. For as technological advances increase the degree of automation in industry, progressively reducing working hours, but at the same time increasing boredom at work, there will be further need to counter the imbalance of unsatisfying employment with satisfying leisure pursuits. How many working people are using their full intellectual or aesthetic potential? Perhaps in the answer to this question lies a clue to much current restlessness and dissatisfaction, and the present education system must accept partial responsibility.

Technological advance is to be welcomed, for it should result in richer productivity, and in the release of man and woman-power to staff the expanding socio-educational services at present stunted and strained by lack of personnel and money.† With the increase of the opportunities for individual learning will come to growing children an awareness that learning is something *you do*— not something you wait to have done *to* you. This latter idea, widespread not only amongst school children but also among students and in the adult world, almost certainly springs from the formative classroom experiences of authoritarian school life, where children's educability is too often assessed by the docility with which they conform to group levels of behaviour and achievement,

* Notably the universities of Keele and of Sussex.

† Shortage of teachers has already been referred to: the demand for educational psychologists outstrips the supply (see footnote, p. 42): paid and voluntary social workers are overworked: "Our Youth Services are still primitive, and they are crippled at this present time by a shortage of Leaders" (Lord Robertson, March 1965).

and education itself by the attainment of paper qualifications. And so, by a circular route, we return to school, where flexibility leads to freer methods and to wider choices, to individual personal responsibility for learning, to social competence and contribution, and, incidentally, to the abandonment of coercion by punishment.

General acceptance of the carry-over of learning into adult life would do much to reduce the existing tensions between adolescent groups and society, manifest in rebellious behaviour and a rise in delinquency. At present, for the majority, the symbol of emergence from dependent childhood is school-leaving, that is the throwing off of disciplinary restrictions, of the learning situation, and, with these, of the idea of learning. Learning is equated with dependence and childhood, and rejected with them: the beginning of independence is thus, for many, coincidental with the end of education.

With the rapid advance of science and technology it becomes imperative that everyone accepts learning as a life-long process. The professional knows the difficulty of keeping up to date: in-service and refresher courses are vital for him. The worker in industry must be prepared to find that his work and skills have become obsolete, perhaps more than once in his lifetime: willingness and opportunity to retrain will give him two, perhaps three prospective careers in a lifetime.

Flexibility in the educational system and individual readiness to adapt and learn throughout life are the essentials of this outlook, which would lessen the gulf between the adult and the adolescent. For if adults be seen making profitable, and, it is to be hoped, pleasurable use of education, the feelings of rebellion against the latter should be modified. At present they are not minimized by a fixed school-leaving age*[10] equated, for the majority, with the end of learning. For others, paper qualifications become the symbol of emergence from childhood into manhood,

* Dr. Tanner, in *Education and Physical Growth*, suggests "getting rid of the school leaving age as such".

and the struggle for them the all-too barren purpose of secondary schooling.

If school-leaving became more flexible, and facilities for further education more readily available and appropriate, and if it were recognized and made explicit that education for all is a life-long process during which retraining and changes of career were not only possible but probable, and through which more facets of personality could be cultivated, the school approach to learning could become altogether more leisurely, with more informed choices of specialization, and a careful re-thinking of the role and relevance of examinations in the system.

EDUCATION AND MENTAL HEALTH

In the field of psychological and mental health there is great need for an extensive programme of investigation into the relationships between home and school, into psycho-social and educational stress and human breakdown, and of guidance for those engaged in educational and social work. Investigations in child guidance clinics and discussions at case conferences are sometimes conducted in an aura of secrecy in which reports and written comments are required from teachers, but there is a minimal feedback to the teacher from the psychologist, medical expert or welfare organization. There is at times a highly exaggerated air of caution and apprehension lest confidential information leak, or an outsider (the teacher) disturb a therapy situation by an incautious word. The confidential nature of the therapy or welfare situation is well understood by the school: however, teachers would appreciate recognition of the fact that they are in daily and influential contact with children whose disturbed behaviour can disrupt the atmosphere of a whole class. As it now is, the teacher attempts to educate the difficult child as best he may, whilst himself often feeling the need of guidance in overcoming the practical problems of the situation. In a word, enlightened co-operation is needed.

Young people and adults also need positive teaching in the study of self-awareness and self-appraisal. Insight into the dynamics and motivations of human behaviour would help them to make more satisfactory adult relationships and to avoid in due course some of the causes of tension in their own children. In turn the children would profit more from their own education and become themselves better parents.

The teacher has special need of psychological insight, since, in the words of Dr. Wall,[11] "there is no member of the community with a heavier responsibility", but opportunity to gain such insight could with advantage be made available to all. Self-understanding would help every individual in the full realization of the worthwhile attributes of his or her own personality. Psychological knowledge has surely reached the point when useful teaching could be given to all young people. A proper programme of recruitment to the profession of educational psychologist* is urgently needed to make available teaching in human behaviour to all children at secondary level.

Alongside such a programme needs to go consideration of twentieth-century feminine status and education. Girls and women, as working members of the community and as home-makers, at present frequently appear to play contradictory roles of responsibility and dependence, leading to stress which may unwittingly be transmitted to their children. Whilst many women need the intellectual satisfaction or financial independence of work outside the home, they also have the fundamentally bio-logical need of support when bringing up young children.

Women themselves are confused about such issues: anxieties and tensions result in psycho-somatic stress, and they and the whole family suffer. An imaginative programme of education for girls including sociological and psychological study could be

---

* March 1965. A committee under the chairmanship of Professor A. Summerfield was set up to consider the qualifications and recruitment of educational psychologists. It is to be hoped that closer liaison with and actual teaching in schools will also come under consideration.

specifically related to their particular abilities, roles and interests, which are not necessarily those of boys. It would add significantly to the narrowly educational purpose (in the sense of subject attainment) of the secondary course for the young adolescent, as well as helping to adjust social malfunctioning and providing insightful guidance for the future.* Some study of sociology, psychology and anthropology would also be invaluable for boys, many of whom ultimately show gross irresponsibility as fathers.†

Writing of the need for the primary school teacher to know "quite a lot about the life of the community", Professor Dobinson,[12] of the University of Reading says: "It is obvious that the best preparation in the sixth forms is a two year course [in sociology and civics] without examination." Such study would widen the horizons, not only of those about to undertake training for teaching but of all secondary school children.

SUMMARY

It seems likely that some of the failures of ineffectual teaching, and also some of the stress states that are causing such concern today, the mental illness, delinquency, maladjustment‡ and criminality may be directly or indirectly caused by the pressures of our inflexible educational system, and that their mitigation may be being hindered by the lack of co-operation in family, social welfare and school life. Certainly they are not lessened by the strain, in some cases, of a too-early start, of attendance for long hours, by the failure and rejection reflected in streaming and the 11+: they are aggravated by lack of further education for the

* Writing of day release courses for girls, F. D. Fowler, Principal of Kingsway Day College, says: "They need to be convinced of the relevance of what they are offered as education to some part of their lives which they can identify for themselves, or to situations in which they believe (or can be convinced) they may find themselves in the future" (*Education*, February 1965).

† "The Salvation Army is preoccupied by the national problem of 885,000 children in families without a father" (from a report in *The Guardian*, 1965).

‡ "Truancy is a form of breakdown with occurs when the stresses imposed upon the child are more than he can bear" (Dr. D. H. Stott, Glasgow University, addressing the Educational Welfare Officers National Association Conference).

academically inadequate, the physically handicapped and the maladjusted and by conflicts in the sometimes over-strained situation of the nuclear family. There needs to be some "tough fundamental re-thinking about the role of the school in the community, the relation between parents and teachers, and the whole purpose of education".*

But schools cannot do this re-thinking alone. Teachers are often too hard pressed for reflection. Social workers, too, are over-strained in patching up the breakdowns of the unfortunate and the misfits: welfare officials are fully engaged in therapeutic and remedial activity.

There is urgent need for the establishment, at high level, of a body wholly concerned with the integration of the various organizations at present operating separately on behalf of children. Apart from the home, there are bodies at present responsible, through the local authorities, to the Department of Education and Science, to the Ministry of Health and to the Home Office. Those who work in them are acutely aware of the many instances when fragmentation of responsibility leads to duplication of work, to misunderstanding, to lack of co-ordination, to wasted time and effort. Meanwhile, the child falls through the mesh.

The setting up, early in 1966, of the Social Services Research Council is warmly welcomed. Let one of its first tasks be, not investigation into the *need* for integration of the home, the school and the services working for the welfare of children, for the need is self-evident. Let it recommend the immediate establishment of a *socio-educational organization* whose urgent purpose will be to further this co-operation in the interests of all children (not only those in evident need†), to create links where there are at present

* Anthony Wedgwood Benn, M.P., writing in *The Guardian*, 1965.

† "Local authority services which have responsibility for children in need—education, welfare and health, should create a Family Advice Service in co-operation with voluntary organisations" (Association of Chief Education Officers' evidence to the Royal Commission on Penal Reform). Also recommended, "In-service training of teachers, particularly secondary school teachers, to develop an awareness of the child as a total personality, not as an IQ only."

gaps, and actively to promote the interfunctioning of schools with homes and the local community.*

Such an integrating body must itself be essentially flexible: its task can never be finalized. The socio-educational system itself must go on evolving, changing as the problems change, and the forces and factors acting upon human beings alter. It is not enough to see what needs doing: we must act in the knowledge that "the future is not simply a projection of past trends, but is also an outcome of what in our time we do to shape it".†

REFERENCES

1. HEMMING, J., Educating Man for Modern Society, New Society, April, 1959.
2. WINNICOTT, D. W., The Child, the Family and the Outside World, Tavistock Publications.
3. DOUGLAS, J. W. B., The Home and the School, MacGibbon & Kee. FLOUD, J. and HALSEY, A. H., Homes and Schools, Educational Research, Vol. 3, No. 2. WALL, W. D., SCHONELL, F. J. and OLSEN, W. C., Failure in School, Unesco, Hamburg.
4. BAKER, J., Children in Chancery, Hutchinson.
5. MUSGROVE, F. and TAYLOR, P. H., Teachers' and Parents' Conception of the Teacher's Role, Brit. Journal of Ed. Psychology, Vol. 35, Pt. 2.
6. GESELL, A. and ILG, F. L., The Child from Five to Ten, Hamish Hamilton.
7. RIDGWAY, L. and LAWTON, I., Family Grouping in the Infants' School, Ward Lock.
8. WILLIAMSON, G. S. and PEARSE, I. H., Science, Synthesis and Sanity, Collins.
9. PATERSON, N., et al., Experiments in Education at Sevenoaks, Constable Young Books, Ltd.
0. TANNER, J. M., Education and Physical Growth, University of London Press.
1. WALL, W. D., Education and Mental Health, Unesco, Harrap. Also Report of a Working Party on the Youth Employment Service (Albermarle), H.M.S.O.
2. DOBINSON, C. M., Schooling, 1963–1970, Harrap.

* The Association of Educational Psychologists, recommending some school changes to the Central Advisory Council for Education refers to "a gross underfunctioning" of the school as a focal point for community interest and activity.

† Renée Mahou, Director-General United Nations Educational, Scientific and Cultural Organization; from an article, Education in 1984, New Scientist, May 1964.

CHAPTER 3

PERSONAL EDUCATION

OWEN WHITNEY*

Formerly Education Secretary of the National Marriage Guidance Council

EDUCATION is the art of the possible. It often triumphs against odds; there are plenty of "confessions" to testify to that. However, the writer on educational theory, whatever his experience to the contrary, must present his argument under optimum (not necessarily ideal) conditions. The validity of an idea can only be tested in such circumstances. In a school community, with its conflicting pressures on time and resources, the teacher seeks to achieve the practicable—and a little more. The theorist, drawing on and distilling the essence of education in its day-to-day setting, indicates potentialities to whose fulfilment the teacher aspires. The latter accomplishes as much as he can, knowing that any theory will have to be modified to fit a particular situation. Fortunately situations are not immutable and do not of themselves defeat an idea which, if tenable and relevant, makes its claims on the school's time and resources. Priorities in education must change with changing needs; otherwise there is danger, as A. N. Whitehead observed, "that education will freeze, and it will be thought, 'this and this are the right things to know', and when this happens thought is dead".[1]

The present chapter discusses the case for personal education—

* Owen Whitney was trained in social work at Oxford and taught backward children for five years. He then turned to adult education and later was for three years Education Secretary to the National Marriage Guidance Council.

here defined as the experiential study of the self in relation to others—in the school context, but its conclusions and recommendations are no less applicable to college and youth club groups. One preliminary point should be mentioned. There are several terms—youth counsellor, education counsellor, youth tutor, group leader—to describe adults who work with young people in the field of personal education. None seems adequate to comprehend this aspect of learning. *Teacher*, with its root meaning, has greater exactness and, moreover, emphasizes the link, in method and philosophy, between personal and other forms of education.

I

THE BACKGROUND

E. M. Forster's novel, *Howard's End*, contains a simple inscription: "only connect . . .". Those two words summarize this chapter and also point to one of the main philosophical and educational questions of our time. The nature and structure of communication engage the attention of the philosopher and in education itself the dialogue (or its absence) between teacher and student is a matter of prime importance. It is the function of the teacher, as Martin Buber has shown, to be responsive to the felt needs of his students by reaching out to them. Real teaching, C. P. Snow commented, "is getting into people, feeling with them".[2] Buber and Snow succinctly described the personal situation which is appropriate to all learning, but it is argued here that the teacher has a further responsibility. To live a dialogue with his pupils is the beginning; from that actual experience—a microcosm of life itself—they have to discover for themselves, reflectively and critically, the meaning and ordering of human relationships. Education is not only dialogue; it is *about* dialogue.

Why the personal concerns the teacher is the immediate theme. Hitherto, with a limited meaning, this has been the province of the moralist and theologian or left to the traditions of family and community. More recently, it has come within the orbit of the biologist, doctor and psychologist. Some indeed would still debate whether the personal world—and its manifestation in human relationships—is, in an educational sense, a recognizable and integrated area of learning. This chapter demonstrates that it is by pursuing three lines of inquiry.

First, the philosophical and social background to the contemporary emphasis on the personal is examined. What developments in philosophical thought and what social changes have occasioned a new focus of interest on the existence *between* people? This analysis indicates that understanding of the personal depends on conditions of learning that are essential in all aspects of education. What, secondly, are those conditions? Finally, it is suggested that existing ways of learning about the personal are inadequate. Wherein lies their inadequacy? These problems define and determine the approach, in method and content, to personal education which is the subject of the second part of the chapter.

Now to the background. Two related changes in philosophy mark an important development in the understanding of the personal. The linguistic school has stressed the primacy of words in comprehending human reality. "Language", John MacMurray has written, "is the major vehicle of communication. Communication is the sharing of experience."[3] Wittgenstein, in his *Philosophical Investigations*, argued that the basic constituents of life could only be perceived through the study of the words that make up the existence between people. Reality, as felt by men, is given content and form through their ability to relate to one another. Language is the main source of that relationship.

Linguistic philosophy drew attention to one aspect of personal relationships—the nature and function of language. John MacMurray himself, in *The Form of the Personal*, added another dimension to knowledge of inter-personal experience. He started from the premise that "there can be no man until there are at least two men in communication".[3] From this point of departure, he criticized traditional philosophy which, he held, was purely theoretical and egocentric. MacMurray claimed that it defined the self only in its reflective activity and as an isolated individual, withdrawn from active relationship with other selves. It was his contribution to transfer the centre of gravity in philosophy from thought to action and, in his own words, "to show how the personal relations of persons is constitutive of personal existence".[3] This philosophical preoccupation with activity (as opposed to egocentric reflection) and with communication gains in significance if seen in its social setting. Ernest Gellner has taken modern philosophers to task for not, in the old-fashioned sense, trying to change the world and guide political life. His *Words and Things* has some pertinent criticisms at that level, but does less than justice to the fact that the interest in language and in human communication illuminates, even if it does not change, two problems of direct personal and social relevance.[4]

First, by its complexity, contemporary society reduces much activity to a functional level. Martin Buber demonstrated, in his *I and Thou*, the tendency for relationships between men to be cast in terms of I–It rather than of I–Thou.[5] The I–It is the negation of the personal in a society which of necessity emphasizes functional processes. That we define a man according to his occupation is, Raymond Williams has said, an indication that his functional role takes pre-eminence over his life and inter-personal world.[6] "What makes modern society so difficult to bear", Hannah Arendt wrote in *The Human Condition*, "is not the number of people involved, or at least not primarily, but that the world between them has lost its powers to gather them together, to relate them and to separate them".[7]

Ours is a largely functional society. To that extent, the philosophical concern with the personal is relevant to the educator who sees his task as helping his students to maintain and enrich their *humanness* in an I–It situation. It also has—and this is the second problem—a bearing on the compensatory activity through which man attempts to overcome his loneliness and loss of identity. The philosophical preoccupation with the personal is mirrored by the accent on relationships in our ordinary lives. In expression it ranges from the starry-eyed, fabricated but powerful sentiments of the popular song to the more considered and person-centred revaluations of marriage and other human institutions. The primacy of persons in this latter sense is reflected, for example, in the greater tolerance towards divorce and pre-marital sex. It implies a questioning of traditional institutions (and of the laws from which they stem) in defining and regulating personal behaviour.

In practice, of course, the principle of contract was both violated and ignored but was none the less accepted as essential to social order. Personal relationships were contained within agreed patterns to which in conscience (and law) the individual was answerable. The Wolfenden Report, however, in its recognition of the *right* to a private area of behaviour abstracted from the community, gave confirmation to the fact that our society, in contradistinction to the Middle Ages, has no longer a pervasive social order, rooted in a collective morality.[8] The order of the past, moreover, was underpinned by a transcendental justification and by secular institutions and sanctions that ensured its enforcement. Explicitly it provided a framework for the ordering of human feelings and relationships.

The decline of traditional forms is part of modern history and its effects on young people were noted in the Albemarle and Crowther Reports. The first of these observed that boys and girls "trying to find their direction without so many customary sign-posts, perhaps without the long-established habits of a steady local life, will be put under special strains".[9] Crowther pointed to two significant trends; "the rise in unsupervized association between teenage boys and girls; and the virtual disappearance of many of the old rules of right and wrong which were formerly accepted even when they were not obeyed."[10]

Because young people are growing up in a world uncertain of its values, without structures of feeling that are explicit, shared and relevant, because at the same time feeling between people has a heightened meaning to the point of being almost the definition of existence itself, personal education assumes a new significance and presents the teacher with a twofold responsibility. He has to take to himself an area of learning which traditionally lay elsewhere or which more recently has become part of an exciting but unreal evaluation of life in the mass media. Within that area of learning he has then to create the conditions in which young people may develop for themselves the capacity to shape and order their experiences of one another.

The problem may be put in three propositions. First, the balance between the content of relationships and the forms appropriate to their expression has been disturbed by a decline in the forms themselves and a complementary increase in the value attached to feeling. Second, this release of feeling—a repudiation of the Anglo-Saxon taboo on tenderness—therefore becomes a matter of inner coherence rather than of social control. Finally, the achievement of this inner coherence is dependent upon an integrated process of learning which, as we shall see later, is in sharp contrast to the fragmented way in which knowledge of the personal is usually received. The next point to consider is: how, in this integrated sense, do we learn?

LEARNING AND PERSONAL GROWTH

Knowledge of the world, both within the self and as a social fact, is a consequence of learning. All experience is a human version of that world. "The brain of each one of us does literally create his or her own world"[6] and "something that happens (in the world) becomes an event only when it is mentally and emotionally perceived and registered."[11] Reality is intelligible when the individual meaningfully organizes his responses to experience. "Life", Piaget has pointed out, "is a continuous creation of increasingly complex forms and a progressive adaptation of these forms to the environment."[12] From a different context, Allport has referred in similar terms to the development of personality.

It is, he wrote, "governed not only by the impact of stimuli upon a slender endowment of drives common to the species. Its process of becoming is governed, as well, by a disposition to realize its possibilities, i.e. to *become* (my italics) characteristically at all stages."[13]

From time immemorial, man has pondered the *nature* of the mind. Broadly his conclusions lie between the polarized views of the English philosopher, John Locke, and the German, Leibniz. Locke assumed the mind to be a *tabula rasa* at birth. He maintained that the intellect itself is passive and acquires content and structure "through the impact of sensation and the criss-cross of association . . . Locke insisted that there can be nothing in the intellect that was not first in the senses".[13] Leibniz amended this theory by agreeing that there is nothing in the intellect that was not first in the senses, *save only the intellect itself*.

In Leibniz's contention, the mind is perpetually active in its own right and according to its own nature, whereas Locke thought it responds only when stimulated. This controversy throws an interesting light on the learning process. Both Locke and Leibniz started from a common assumption—that learning and therefore growth result from the activity of the mind in its encounter with the environment. The mind learns and grows through its own receptivity to experience.

To be effective, a learning process is dependent upon four conditions. First, it is dependent upon the quality of the environment—the perceptual field—to which the individual is exposed. The range of available experience will affect the rate and quality of growth. In respect of young children Casler has advanced the hypothesis of *perceptual* deprivation as being more relevant to intellectual and emotional development than the better-known concept of *maternal* deprivation.[14] In *Intelligence and Experience* Hunt concluded that house-proud parents may hinder the development of their children, even lower their final level of intelligence by the restriction of their activity.[15]

Second, learning is both an interactive and out-going process

It is not simply the taking in of knowledge. Readers of Muriel Spark will recall the essential difference between Miss Jean Brodie and the Headmistress of the Marcia Blaine School.

> The word "education" [Miss Brodie explained to her set] comes from the root *e* from *ex*, out, and *duco*, I lead. It means a leading out. To me education is a leading out of what is already there in the pupil's soul. To Miss Mackay it is a putting in of something that is not there, and that is not what I call education, I call it intrusion, from the Latin prefix *in* and meaning in and the stem *trudo*, I thrust. Miss Mackay's method is to thrust a lot of information into the pupil's head; mine is a leading out of knowledge, and that is true education as is proved by the root meaning.[16]

Third, Piaget's concept of the continuous creation of increasingly complex forms was quoted earlier. A new structure of knowledge must be integrated to its predecessors if the individual is to build up a coherent picture of the world. Newman, in his *On the Scope and Nature of University Education*, has argued that growth

> consists, not merely in the passive reception into the mind of a number of ideas hitherto unknown to it, but in the mind's energetic and simultaneous action upon and towards and among these new ideas which are rushing in upon it. It is the action of a formative power, reducing to order and meaning the matter of our acquirements; it is a making of the objects of our knowledge subjectively our own . . . a digestion of what we receive into the substance of our previous state of thought. . . . There is no enlargement, unless there be a comparison of ideas one with another, as they come before the mind, and a systematizing of them.[17]

Newman's words stand eloquently without comment.

Finally, "individuals are unique, through a particular heredity expressed in a particular history", but they are only human in so far as they are able to communicate with one another.[6] Our separate perceptions of the world must share some common content and structures. It is the plight of the autistic child that he lacks the capacity for communion; he fails to connect through growth and learning. The same is no less true of the schizophrenic.[18]

These four conditions determine the quality of learning and personal growth. The capacity to learn varies from individual to individual, but all are involved in similar processes of perception, response and assimilation. If life, as Piaget suggests, consists of the continuous creation of forms that owe their origin to these processes, where outside the self does the individual select the raw material from which the forms are constructed? What, in other words, are the avenues of learning? Do these avenues make up a perceptual field that is adequate for understanding the personal world?

THE AVENUES OF LEARNING

In respect of academic and technical subjects, similar questions would scarcely need asking. Within an established or developing tradition which includes material, language and method, essential conditions for learning are duly expected. The student accepts the discipline of his chosen field and recognizes that valid knowledge does not result from rote learning or from an unquestioning adherence to untested assumptions, facts and theories. Rather it is the consequence of the activity of his own mind in subjecting his material to creative and critical scrutiny. It is the drawing out from the self to which Miss Brodie referred. At the same time, according to the level of his work and intelligence, he may evolve new ideas and meanings which extend the boundaries of that discipline.

The student is further aware that in the acquisition of knowledge he can only move forward by grasping the significance of each step in turn and by relating it to what he has learnt already. Otherwise his thought has the syncretism which, as Piaget has shown, characterizes the child's first explorations of reality.[19] Finally, the student needs to be part of a community of learning and to share in the forms and language appropriate to that community.

Clearly, not all learning situations completely fulfil these conditions but they remain the aspirations on which the most searching intellectual and creative work is likely to be based. In contrast how do we come to know the personal world? What are the conditions of learning in this sphere of human experience? One important difference is immediately obvious. In both the sciences and the humanities, there is an emotional involvement but also a detachment and objectivity that derive from the subject discipline itself. The student gets inside his work; he must be able to stand outside as well. In personal education, he—and the teacher—is intimately part of his field of inquiry. It is not easy for him to escape the subjectivity imposed by his own experience of life. A first essential for him is to come to terms with the influences within himself that affect time present and time future.[20]

At the beginning of this chapter, it was suggested that hitherto teaching about the personal has been in the hands of the moralist and theologian and that more recently it has been the concern of the biologist, doctor and psychologist. How have these specialists discharged their responsibilities? Their contribution and limitations require examination before the case for another approach is put. These formal avenues of learning are not the only, or even the most important, sources of knowledge about human relationships and it is necessary to look also at the informal and largely unconscious ways in which the young person builds up a picture of the personal world.

Two preliminary distinctions should be stated. First, all avenues of learning, apart from the mass media, depend to some extent on direct contact with people—peer group adolescents, parents, teachers, doctors or clergymen. Learning will be affected by the quality of these relationships. A child from a loving family will know something different from one who is continually shunted from one set of foster parents to another. Equally two biology teachers may elicit contrasted responses from their students, even though they are handling similar material. In the immediate context, the avenues of learning are being examined, not the people who are responsible for their transmission. A skilful teacher can transcend the limitations of a medium, but this does not validate the medium itself. The transcendence is an indication of the teacher's exceptional quality—his ability to rise above restricting circumstances. The avenues of learning about the personal must be judged on their intrinsic merits.

Secondly, there is a distinction between what is offered in a learning situation and what in fact the students actually assimilate. The real value of a situation is in proportion to its fulfilment of the felt needs of those present. A comprehensive coverage of a subject from the teacher's point of view will not necessarily satisfy those for whom, in good faith, it is intended. We listen, but do not always hear because the teacher has failed to touch something within us. An avenue is only acceptable provided that its stimulus answers a need and produces a related response.

Informal learning is the most influential. Other forms are amplifications, additions and modifications to this primary source of the personal. It has two aspects; the incorporation into the self of actual lived experience; and the traditions in the immediate environment which shape and regulate human behaviour.

From the researches of John Bowlby and others, there is general agreement that emotional experiences in the early years of life determine the child's capacity to relate, both qualitatively and quantitatively, to other people.[21] Ernest Jones once said that preparation for marriage begins at birth. He meant that the existence between an infant and its parents is the blue-print for the total picture of relationships that emerges throughout life.

The child's vision of the personal originates in his own family and then extends to other people who have greater or lesser contact with him. From this network, he empirically deduces its nature and gradually organizes his transitory impulses to relate into a structured reality of feelings—love, hate, loyalty, sympathy. He is born, Ian Suttie has suggested, with an innate propensity to love and relate which, through the process of *affective evolution*, is the basis for his socialization into a communicating person.[22] The quality of his life—his perceptual field in the emotional sense—determines the extent to which he can realize that innate propensity. From the flow of feeling, positive or negative, in his own situation, he learns to respond appropriately. He loves through first being loved.

The organization of the personal into a coherent picture involves an affective evolution from direct experience. That is one aspect of informal learning. As the child constructs his own version of reality, he will become aware that his environment contains attitudes, customs and expectations with which he is expected to comply. He creates an individual world, but as part of a wider framework which will limit the form and content of that world—unless he dwells in asocial and amoral fantasies. His growth depends upon an initial acceptance of the mores that order the life of the community, even if he comes later to question and reject some of them. Tradition is the second aspect of informal learning; it has two important characteristics.

First, the customs and patterns of behaviour in a family or community, as perceived by the child, have an implicit assumption of rightness which—initially at least—is not to be challenged. It is the *known* about human behaviour. The child grows up to believe in his way of life. Therefore—and this is the second characteristic—it is the reference point for evaluating other interpretations of human behaviour. When the child is capable of reflective thought, he will see that many customs and obligations are socially convenient rationalizations which may bear little relevance to the experience he knows from life itself. It is not just that he attunes to the compromises of his elders. Long before he may be suffused with guilt for feelings and actions that seem to stray outside the established pattern. Very early in his life he has to face the conflict between the world he knows inwardly and the social approximation outside.

Traditions have the function of providing an external framework for the organization and control of behaviour between persons. Moral teachings, the first of the formal avenues of learning, have the same function. Since the time of St. Paul, the church has claimed the right to legislate for human conduct. From the pulpit, at Sunday School, and in the ordinary classroom, children in our society learn the Christian ethic of personal relationships. It is called Christian but, as I have pointed out elsewhere, it owes more in its evaluation of the personal to St. Paul than to the founder of the religion himself.[23] Apart from the general injunction to love (this comes undisputedly from Christ), the church has tended to emphasize the negative aspects of relationships, especially in that between man and woman. In addition, it has taught morality as an external system of restraints rather than as a more positive loving from which consideration for others follows. It has associated sex with sin and implanted the fear that feeling must be controlled from without and not ordered inwardly. To this end, chastity has always been defined as a prohibition against the expression of feeling rather than its refinement.[24]

As with community traditions, moral teachings are imbued with the inevitability of rightness. The Newsom Report, for example, reaffirmed unquestioningly the principle of chastity before marriage and fidelity within it.[25] The ethical conflict, to which reference has already been made, had for the committee but one solution—the restoration of an established view. That view was not apparently open to critical scrutiny, despite the revaluations within and outside the church.[26] In its endorsement of tradition, the Newsom Committee drew attention to an important fact about moral systems. Whatever their origins or justification, they do not take into account the reality—in terms of ordinary living—of the actual existence between people. Indeed they can do precisely the reverse by distorting or denying that experience. For this reason the idea of an external moral law, immutable and unrelenting, is at variance with the modern concept of persons which recognizes the diversity of human need and experience.

The veil of secrecy over discussion of man–woman relationships in our society is too well known to require elaboration here. The breakthrough—this has become the second avenue of formal learning about the personal—was an attempt to give to young people fundamental information about human biology and reproduction. After a number of tentative beginnings, it is now practice common to many schools to run courses on human development. The value of such instruction is not disputed but, as a means of communicating learning about life, it is deficient in at least two respects. First, the approach does little to evoke the poetry of creation; second, it tends to be embarrassingly primitive. John Wilson, in his *Logic and Sexual Morality*, has written: "few things could be more unnatural than, for instance, the sketchy and formalized diagrams labelled 'the female reproductive system' or 'the male generative organs'. Children want to know . . . what the sexual anatomy of human beings *actually looks like*. For this purpose photographs would be better than diagrams, and a visible illustration from real life better than either."[27] With Dr. Wilson, it is relevant to ask whether a more evocative and scientific method of teaching might have greater meaning to the many boys and girls who leave school with an inadequate understanding of the working of their own bodies.

The third avenue is the medical approach. Some local authorities and individual schools consider doctors and medical officers of health to be the most appropriate persons to instruct the young on problems of growth and maturation and therefore of relationships. It is undeniable that a doctor will possess accurate knowledge of the human anatomy and, in another way, be up to date with contraception and the treatment of venereal disease. Does this professional competence, clearly essential in his role of doctor, equip him, however, to deal with the totality of experience involved in human relationships? Is a medical orientation too clinical? Does it too readily associate natural healthy development with illness and treatment? The answer to such questions will, as was pointed out before, depend largely upon the calibre of a specialist as a *person*, but the medical approach in itself does leave unexpressed much of what young people know intuitively and experientially in their own lives. In that sense it does not connect with their experience.

Biology and medicine are by definition centred in the workings and reactions of the body as it develops towards maturity. They have no direct connection with the psychology of human growth, but this aspect of learning is no less important for understanding personal relationships. The study of psychology has added another dimension to teaching and it is becoming practice also to integrate this study into the work of older pupils in secondary schools. That young people should know something of psychology is desirable—it is the fourth avenue of learning about the personal world—but its value is limited if it is presented in a straight and formal way without reference to their own living experience of growing up. It is not, for example, enough to discuss the Oedipus situation or sibling rivalry in purely intellectual terms and without a genuine and searching examination of the self.

There remains one other avenue of learning about the personal, the mass media. Much material for television, film, magazine-type literature and popular song originates in what purport to be real-life situations but in fact they provide a two-dimensional and over-simplified version of the human condition. In discussion of television, Bruno Bettelheim has suggested that its content is less a cause for concern than "what persistent watching does to a child's ability to relate to real people, to become self-activating, to think on the basis of his own life experience instead of in stereo-types out of shows".[28] Richard Hoggart has, in a further criticism of the media, pointed out that "life is full of problems on which we have—or feel we should try—to make decisions, as citizens or as private individuals. But neither the real difficulty of these decisions, nor their true and disturbing challenge to each individual, can often be communicated through the mass media."[29] The media give little insight into real people; rather they rely, for obvious commercial reasons, either on devitalized and "safe" concepts of human life or on an exploitation and vulgarization of our sexual and aggressive tendencies. Their importance, however, is not to be ignored. As I. A. Richards wrote forty or more years ago: "bad literature, bad art and the cinema, etc., are an influence of the first importance in fixing immature and actually inapplicable attitudes to most things.

Even the decision as to what constitutes a pretty girl or a handsome young man, an affair apparently natural and personal enough, is largely determined by magazine covers and movie stars."[30]

The child learns about the personal world both informally, from actual experience and from the traditions of family and community life in which he is nurtured, and formally through the teachings of morality and religion, biology, medicine and psychology. In addition, the mass media have a pervasive effect in shaping his understanding of human life and relationships. Something of the particular limitations of these avenues of learning has already been indicated. How far, in fact, do they, in furthering awareness of the personal, comply with the essential conditions of learning? Do they provide an *education* in human relationships?

Actual experience is the raw material of personal education but its construction into a coherently human version of reality is a learning process dependent upon those essential conditions. In two senses these avenues of learning can claim to contribute towards the creation of that version of reality. First, both local traditions and formal morality offer an external framework for the ordering of human behaviour. And secondly, the biological, medical and psychological approaches to the personal give the very relevant factual basis to relationships.

The contribution at these levels is, however, limited. An external code of behaviour as has been indicated, cannot by definition take account of the diversity of human need and experience; traditional morality has disintegrated precisely because of this inadequacy. Bereft of the sanctions which ensured its enforcement and increasingly vulnerable to criticism, its influence on personal relationships is now less clearly evident. Its unquestioning reaffirmation, in an ethically fragmented world, confuses rather than helps the young. As one commentator said: hitherto "we have lived under the *law*. What we are asked to do now is to live under *grace*. That is what the new morality means."[31]

The problem is to fashion an education that will enable the young to respond to this dispensation.

Information about human physiology and psychology is integral to an understanding of personal relationships, but it is the raw material for comprehending the existence between people. It is not the existence itself and has to be woven into the thoughts and feelings of young people as they grow up. Cognitive knowing is not the same, or as important, as meaningful reflection on what is happening experientially to oneself.

Insight into a technical or academic subject depends upon an awareness of both its structure and content within the essential conditions of learning. It is no less relevant to consider the totality of the existence between people, but learning of the personal tends to be fragmented, contradictory and inadequately structured. The mass media distort and simplify; tradition and morality probe the problem of external order, but do not explore the intensely individual and unconscious motivation in human behaviour. The professional approaches through biology, medicine and psychology make reference to separate aspects of personal growth. Moreover, each emphasizes the teaching of something rather than the drawing out of the potentiality for communication and relationship which Suttie claimed is inherent in humanity. A unified approach to personal education is the theme of the second half of this chapter.

II

The aim of personal education is to help young people understand and order their experience of human relationships in an emotionally charged and unstable world. The problem is to discover how learning of the personal, at present haphazard and fragmented, can be made more effective and relevant to them. To start with, as the above analysis has indicated, this learning is the province of the educator. Personal growth or affective evolution is not an organic process solely dependent upon *natural* laws; nor is it simply amenable to external control; rather it is a dynamic aspect of development responsive to the dialogue of education.

Secondly, personal education exists in its own right and must be afforded the respect and integrity that characterize other spheres of learning. It is not an eclectic "subject" distributed piecemeal among specialists whose contribution, the sum total of their various competences, is incomplete and lacking in wholeness. *Knowing* the personal involves the emergence of language and forms that adequately comprehend the affective life. Human feelings, as G. H. Bantock sharply observed, are not measured in terms of animal behaviour or positivist philosophy, but articulated and interpreted in concepts that symbolize their intrinsic qualities. [32]

Personal education draws its raw material from the emotions. Existence between people consists of positive, negative and neutral feelings. Emotions are central to the personal world, but, on the one hand, they are distrusted as "tiresome nuisances which need to be sublimated in fantasy or repressed". [32] Seen as a threat to intellectual effort, the belief still persists that boys and girls work better apart, despite the evidence to the contrary. [33] On the other hand, simply to show feeling, whatever its quality, is taken as a sign of warmth and humanity. It is not, however, emotion as such that is peculiar to man—he shares many of its manifestations with animals. The unique human attribute lies in the capacity to articulate feeling in symbolic ways. Man is, Ernest Cassirer remarked, *animal symbolicum*. He has the potentiality to refine and enrich emotion in the context of relationships or artistic forms.

Personal education in fact has close affinities with creative processes. Susanne Langer, in her *Feeling and Form*, has concluded that "sheer self-expression requires no artistic form"; similarly emotion of itself does not constitute the personal world between persons. [34] "Art", she continues, "is the creation of forms symbolic of human feeling." [34] Here there is an exact analogy. Just as art has an expressive function, the articulation of feelings through the process of what Langer calls *objectification*, meaningful and whole relationships have their source in ordered and communicable emotions. Music, Langer has postulated, is "the formulation and representation of emotions, moods, mental tensions and resolutions—a 'logical picture' of sentiment, responsive life, a source of insight, not a plea for sympathy".[34] I know no more concise definition of personal education.

How can it be achieved? The Newsom Report stressed the responsibility of the school in preparing young people for marriage and family life and it is the teacher's role in this respect that will now be discussed. Consideration of personal education in a practical sense poses three main questions: What should be its content? How should it be given? Who should give it? Each of these problems will be examined in turn. They provide the basis from which, it is argued, the young person is able to construct and order his unique but communicable version of reality.

CONTENT

The content of personal education raises the least number of difficulties. Much information about human development is already available; the trouble is that it comes to young people in a diffuse and sometimes contradictory way. It is therefore necessary to outline an integrated programme which will take into account the substance of the specialist approaches referred to earlier in this chapter. Such a programme must be based on the needs of the young people and not on *a priori* assumptions about what they ought to be told. If education means, as Buber has written, "to let a selection of the world affect a person through the medium of another person", it is the teacher who is finally responsible for the selection, but he is guided and limited by the *otherness* of his students.[35]

A programme in personal education is not a syllabus to which a group is expected to adhere literally and in chronological sequence. It is no more than a description of the areas of human experience that are likely to be relevant to young people in their formative adolescent years. In the present chapter, the outline suggests the subjects and problems with which a teacher in personal education should himself be familiar. Its source lies in the questions raised in discussion groups by young people themselves. For convenience, the content is listed under four main headings, although none is, of course, an exclusive category.

Human Physiology. Personal education, derived from a comprehension of feeling, begins with an awareness of the physiological changes that occur *pari passu* with emotional development. Growth at adolescence, in all its manifestations, is the immediate concern, but the interest and curiosity of young people extends back to the origins of life and forward to old age and death. Experienced teachers would, however, agree that, despite their interest, young people often have only a vague and inaccurate knowledge of the structure and functioning of the human organism. The first requirement for the teacher is to have this information which he is able to express in an appropriate and communicable form.[36]

Human Psychology. Secondly, young people are eager to understand motivation in human behaviour. In this respect no teacher can expect to acquire a professional competence in psychology, but it is possible for him to grasp the underlying principles which are used in evaluating why people act and react in particular ways. The frequently asked general question "Why do people . . .?" has many variants and is probably an indirect and therefore tolerable approach to a personal anxiety. The teacher, as will be discussed in a moment, will encourage members of a group to tease out the question in terms of their own experience, but his own contribution gains in value if he has both the capacity to reflect on his own biography and possesses insights from the study of psychology. Relevant knowledge about psychology is fortunately not tucked away in learned monographs.[37]

Moral Issues. Personal education, as we have seen, involves moral issues. These range from straight questions to the teacher about his own views—abortion and homosexuality are perennial subjects—to inquiries about the attitudes of the churches to these and allied problems. Discussion of the ethics of human behaviour calls for an important distinction between facts and inferences. This point becomes clear from an example. Very little is known about the effects of different kinds of sexual behaviour. The influence of pre-marital sexual experience on the stability of marriage varies considerably—the evidence is highly contradictory—but it engenders strong and dogmatic opinions which masquerade as verifiable facts with a universal validity. The teacher has to be conversant with the material of moral controversy and at the same time be able to distinguish between the known and the inferred. Here his own emotional involvement will determine the extent of his objectivity—a point that will be examined more closely later. [38]

Practical Problems. Finally, young people often bring practical inquiries to a discussion. Again these cover numerous topics— anything from the "rights" of children in law, to careers and wedding etiquette. [39]

METHOD

Learning in an academic subject is not dependent simply on the accumulation of facts. Similarly, it is not the intention in personal education "to put across" as much of the above content as possible. Facts known congnitively are only abstract descriptions of the world as it is perceived by the individual. The real substance of personal education is experience and its method is therefore to draw out a response which forms the basis to which new learning is assimilated. The point of departure is not a prescribed syllabus, but the teacher's effort to reach over to the young people in his group so that they are able to articulate their needs, aspirations and anxieties. His task is to contrive a situation which facilitates all the stages of learning in turn. First there is the group setting itself in which, in Langer's phrase, sheer self expression occurs. This is then converted into an ordered and shared experience. Lastly, the individual members absorb the experience to themselves and thereby confirm, modify or recreate their own particular versions of reality. What methods are applicable to this process of learning?

Before a full answer to that question is possible, it is necessary to consider some of the practical details of the setting in which personal education is carried out. The word *group* indicates its form. In the school it suggests greater flexibility than *class* and in fact most classes (other than in the sixth form) are too large for discussion purposes. While a group must have sufficient "voices" to give a range of expressions from which shared experience is drawn, and to provide emotional support for its members, dialogue and learning will only occur in an atmosphere where individuals feel *rapport* with one another and where the leader can be reasonably alert to the needs of everyone present. For these reasons, it is practicable to have a group of about ten to fifteen members with one discussion leader.

As much of the dialogue in personal education has to do with the existence between men and women, it is preferable to work with boys and girls together unless circumstances dictate otherwise. Age is also an important factor in achieving both balance and development in a discussion. Little is effected if there is a wide discrepancy, not so much in chronological age, as in level of emotional maturity. If, for example, a class of 15–16-year-old boys and girls is divided into two sections for personal education, at least two criteria are relevant in making up the separate groups; selection according to sex and according to the stage of emotional development.

The teacher must trust to his own judgement in choosing boys and girls who will collectively form a viable group. This does not mean just pairing off those who get on well together or who can guarantee to get an "argument" started. What will happen in a group cannot be predicted before it goes into action, but it is worth trying to plan for a variety of responses that will together produce a rich perceptual field. Such anticipation is only possible when the teacher already knows the boys and girls well. Otherwise he will have to trust to more spontaneous impressions.

Dialogue, with the concomitant articulation of feeling and its fusion into shared and individual experience, rarely occur immediately. A group may meet several times before it reaches beyond the level of what Bantock has called *discursive language*.[32] Learning in personal education is a gradual and unfolding process dependent upon the amount of time available and upon a continuity of membership. Not much can be achieved in fewer than four to six sessions or with a group that has a continually changing personnel. In the preliminary meeting, time is taken up with overcoming anxiety, diffidence and curiosity before genuine communication is established. From knowing and trusting the leader and one another, the members of the group develop the freedom and flexibility to express their deeper feelings. In the school setting, a double-period is normally suitable in length for a session.

The setting should itself contribute towards purposeful but informal activity in the group. A small room is preferable to a large one; a circle of chairs—armchairs if possible—is better than a classroom arrangement with its rows of desks and the teacher isolated out in front. The teacher is responsible for the group but his *authority* does not separate him from the others. The nearest equivalent is a sixth-form seminar.

As in counselling and psychotherapy, personal education involves the articulation of facts and feelings which in other circumstances would remain hidden from the teacher. He should assure the group that their deliberations are confidential. When something is revealed that calls for action, the point can be discussed privately afterwards with the young person concerned. Fear usually occasions silence; once a problem has been brought out in the warm and supportive atmosphere of a closed group, the young person has begun to face it and is likely to be more willing to accept help.

Now to method. One point has already been implied. Informality is a first requirement in encouraging responses from the group. The corollary to informality is flexibility. As no definite syllabus is laid down, the teacher is free to explore with the group the problems that interest them, provided of course that the discussion is worthwhile and not a "front" to avoid something of more profound concern. Most discussions begin at a neutral and superficial level, but a dynamic group will gradually move into a deeper key.

How does a discussion start? No general rule is applicable and there are several variables to take into account. How intelligent and articulate are the members? Are they used to group discussion? How many sessions are available? How long is each meeting? Is the group familiar with the content of personal education? The teacher himself will obviously expect to open the first session. Depending on the group, he can simply explain the purpose of the course, invite comment and see what happens. An initial silence may follow, but an experienced teacher will not rush in to fill it with words. As he senses the atmosphere of the group, he will come to distinguish a pause that contributes to growth through non-verbal communication and one which inhibits it. Periods of silence are integral to a Bruckner symphony; they also belong to group processes. The value of music does not rest only in its notes.

Or the teacher may begin with an outline of the kind of problem that *could* be examined in the group. With this approach, it is useful to throw out a rhetorical question or refer to a situation in literature that illuminates the problem raised.[40] The technique works well with fairly mature boys and girls who are nevertheless not accustomed to free discussion. Others, raw both to discussion and to the idea of personal education, will probably benefit initially from a straight talk on human development. Such a talk will, however, lose its value if it is delivered as a lecture. A pause or comment after each important point makes for clarity and helps to bring the members early into the practice of discussion. Questions and comment on the introductory talk are the first step towards the original contributions which the teacher will hope later to draw from the boys and girls in the group.

This is the basis from which the members will come to express their thoughts and feelings freely. As in all learning situations, the teacher's reactions to these initial responses will determine the extent to which they will be able to make the transition from discursive language to a more personal level of exploration and communication. When a factual question merges into an opinion or reflection, it is well to remember that the young people are interpreting their own experiences and backgrounds. Their utterances are valid to them, no matter how crude or "wrong" they may appear to anyone else. A young person will go further if his first comments are encouraged by the teacher and then subjected to open but friendly scrutiny by the group. A critical evaluation of this kind has three aspects which can be summarized in three questions. After the teacher has taken up a comment or opinion from a member, it is relevant to ask: Why do you think that? Next the views of the group may be brought out by: does anyone disagree with what has just been said? Finally, the member should have the opportunity to come back if he wished to do so. This is, of course, a simplification of what is often a complicated dialectic but it does contain the essence of the process.

Destructive criticism or a display of superior knowledge or morality by the teacher will either inhibit the group or drive it into a position of permanent hostility. Negative feelings add to the quality of a group only when they are amenable to conversion into something more positive. Then they play an important role to work through tension is a salutary learning process, but immutable attitudes kill any chance of dialogue. It is tempting to cut across views that seem ridiculous or even harmful, but criticism, modification and refinement carry more conviction if the arise from within the group rather than as an "expert" statement from the teacher. On many occasions, it is true, he will be the source of reference for clarification, correction and reformulation but again with patience much of this will come from the young people themselves.

Morally dogmatic pronouncements about human behaviour have no part in personal education, but in the contemporary wasteland of broken convictions the demand for a reaffirmation of traditional beliefs is, as we have seen, strong. Professor Niblett has indicated an important distinction between moral education and moral instruction. "An act", he wrote, "only becomes moral if it involves conscious choice."[38] Moral education is concerned with the development of the capacity to choose; moral instruction transmits an established order, unquestioned and unchanged. In personal education, from an exploration of views, the young people learn decision making for themselves. The choice is not with the teacher.

Expression is the beginning and not the whole of the learning process. The word *choice* suggests the next stage. Earlier in this chapter, it was argued—from the work of Martin Buber—that the teacher has the responsibility to select and limit the educational field in accordance with the needs of the group. From the members' participation, he moulds the relevant and significant individual utterances into a coherent group experience. The shaping of this order will result from the teacher's sensitivity—through words, gestures or apposite silence—to the spoken and unspoken feelings of those present. The perception that will disentangle, select, refine and then fuse these into a meaningful whole is a creative act. It demands from the teacher both objectivity to the needs of the group and emotional *rapport* with its members.

The form and content of the group experience have their origin in the teacher's selection and ordering of individual responses. This is the penultimate stage in learning. What finally matters is the extent to which the participants—including the teacher—absorb it to their own lives. Newman long ago recognized that the dynamic and continuous fusion of new to existing knowledge is a problem of individual mental and emotional activity. The learning situation will, however, contribute to its quality. Through the group, young people develop a language and conceptual framework that is appropriate to discussion and private reflection on the personal world. They learn, as it were, the grammar: the words and formulations used shape their awareness of their own responses to life. Ideally the dialogue of personal education achieves a blend of exactness and poetry. In this respect, it is worth remembering Eliot's dictum: "every precise emotion tends towards an intellectual formulation": and Parry's: "the instinct of utterance makes it a necessity to find terms which will be understood by other beings".[41]

The substance of personal education, save at the factual level, reaches towards no definite conclusions and, in modern jargon, is open-ended. A discussion that "agrees" anything has an air of unimpeachable finality which seems to preclude further examination. Education exists to open hearts and minds, not to confine them. A group is an experience of intrinsic value, but at the same time it is a stimulus to further and continuing emotional and mental activity. A discussion is most effective if it leaves its participants with unresolved questions which provide, not just food for thought, but which also weave themselves into the experience of life itself.

Finally, each of us lives a private nightmare about some aspects of the personal world. We all have thoughts and actions which are scarcely admitted to consciousness because, in the traditions on which we have been nurtured, they are thought to be perverse or peculiar to oneself. Masturbation, for example, has always produced isolated guilt and suffering. Hidden feelings distort and fragment personal development. Through group experience, the individual comes to realize that he shares many practices and anxieties with others. The fact that he is not alone (or if he is, that he has a supportive setting in which to come to terms with his difference) encourages him to face problems from which by himself he had shied away. Communication with the group is the prelude to a creative internal dialogue which in its turn leads to integrated knowledge of the self and of the self in relation to others.

THE LEADER OF THE GROUP

In its aim to help young people to develop the insight to order their experience of life, the value of personal education is measured by the extent to which the members of a group have been able to enter into dialogue with one another and to learn as a consequence. What is the teacher's contribution to this learning process? What kind of teacher is likely to be most effective in personal education? By implication, both questions have already been answered in the above discussion, but they do require further elaboration. Basically, the teacher has the task of facilitating learning by encouraging and guiding the young person's responses. His role is primarily that of commentator and interpreter of the group's activity. As the poet Keats said in another context: "Man should not dispute or assert but whisper results to his neighbour."[42] Therein lies the teacher's responsibility in personal education.

His responsibility is similar in other branches of learning, but through the nature of its subject matter, personal education has an important difference. Its concern with life itself affects the teacher personally no less than the students. They are all involved intellectually and emotionally in the process. The teacher's experience and attitudes—whether explicitly articulated or not—are a part of personal education, and are therefore potentially vulnerable. Vulnerability tends to produce defensive reactions—either aggression or withdrawal—which are inimical to the group experience. Not everyone, it has to be admitted, is able to tolerate situations in which he or she feels emotional pressure or rejection.

Personal education is clearly the vocation of the teacher who has the emotional maturity to accept and respond openly to the needs of others who are struggling towards a coherence of their thoughts and feelings. Maturity does not mean unquestioning certainty, but an integration of heart and mind that allows further growth and receptivity. Its hallmark is the capacity not to be thrown off balance or unnerved by attitudes and behaviour that seem to threaten one's own orientation to life. Related to this equanimity is the flexibility to learn in the light of experience and the recognition of the relativity of one's view of the personal world. Intellectual awareness is not enough; more important is the conviction that one's own standards, whatever their intrinsic merit, are not necessarily shared by others. Proselytizing has no place in personal education, but tolerance is central to it.

There is a growing accumulation of practice, by teachers and education counsellors, which suggests that emotional maturity (in the sense outlined above), flexibility and tolerance are the qualities essential for personal education. In addition, it calls for an intellectual grasp of the various elements that make up a group situation. The teacher has to be able to respond to a diversity of utterances and at the same time select those that are emotionally and intellectually relevant.

Beyond these qualities, other matters are of secondary importance. It is perhaps rare for very young teachers to have had sufficient experience for a sphere of learning that is life itself. Personal education, except at the factual level, has no special connection with any academic or technical subject. A qualification in biology is not of itself a qualification for this work. Nor is geography, but a man or woman who happens to be a geography specialist could be a good teacher in personal education. Like all creative activity, personal education is an art based both on inspiration and technical competence. The intangible quality which translates notes into music or fragmented utterances into a coherent group experience, has little directly to do with training and practice, but through actually doing the work and reflecting on it the teacher will refine and improve his technical competence and develop his insight.

CONCLUSION

The survey *Youth Today* concluded that the great majority of boys and girls "are bred true and, with proper guidance, will contribute as much to the future as their parents are doing now".

In effect the survey refuted the commonly held assumption that the present generation requires "special" treatment by virtue of its shortcomings and difficulties. The term *problem* is so often associated with the young as to suggest that it is inescapably a true description of their condition. Their needs are not to be denied. They must, however, be related, not to untenable generalizations about moral decline and delinquency, but to their potentialities for emotional growth and relationship. This is precisely the emphasis in personal education. As D. W. Winnicott neatly put: "there exists only one real cure for adolescence; maturation".[43]

REFERENCES

1. PIERCE, L., *Dialogues of A. N. Whitehead.*
2. BUBER, M., *Between Man and Man.* SNOW, C. P., *The Search.*
3. MACMURRAY, J., *The Form of the Personal*, Vol. 2—*Persons in Relation.*
4. GELLNER, E., *Words and Things*, MEHTA, V., *Fly and the Fly Bottle.*
5. BUBER, M., *I and Thou.*
6. WILLIAMS, R., *The Long Revolution.*
7. ARENDT, H., *The Human Condition.*
8. The Wolfenden Report on *Homosexuality and Prostitution*, in recommending that homosexual practices between consenting adults should no longer be a criminal offence, argued that there is an area of behaviour which is private and should be beyond the reach of any external law. For criticism of the Wolfenden thesis, see DEVLIN, LORD PATRICK, *The Enforcement of Morals.*
9. *Albemarle Report on the Youth Services.*
10. *Crowther Report*, 15 *to* 18, Vol. 1.
11. HELLER, E., *The Disinherited Mind.*
12. PIAGET, J., *The Origins of Intelligence in Children.*
13. ALLPORT, G., *Becoming.*
14. CASLER, L., *Maternal Deprivation*—a critical review of the literature; quoted in NIBLETT, W. R., *How and Why Do we Learn?*
15. HUNT, J. McV., *Intelligence and Experience.*
16. SPARK, M., *The Prime of Miss Jean Brodie.*
17. NEWMAN, J. H., *On the Scope and Nature of University Education.*
18. LAING, R., *The Divided Self.*
19. PIAGET, J., *The Child's Conception of Reality.*
20. ELIOT, T. S., *The Four Quartets: Burnt Norton.*
21. BOWLBY, J., *Maternal Care and Mental Health.*
22. SUTTIE, I., *The Origins of Love and Hate.*
23. WALKER, K. and WHITNEY, O., *The Family and Marriage in a Changing World.*
24. MACMURRAY, J., *Reason and Emotion.*
25. NEWSOM REPORT, *Half Our Future.*

26. ROBINSON, J., *Honest to God*. RHYMES, CANON, *No New Morality: Towards a Quaker View of Sex*.
27. WILSON, J., *Logic and Sexual Morality*.
28. BETTELHEIM, B., *The Informed Heart*.
29. HOGGART, R., *Mass Communications in Great Britain* in *The Pelican Guide to English Literature*, Vol. 7.
30. RICHARDS, I. A., *Principles of Literary Criticism*.
31. DREWETT, J., quoted in *The Times*, 19 August 1963.
32. BANTOCK, G. H., *Education and Values*.
33. MARRIS, P., *The Experience of Higher Education*.
34. LANGER, S., *Feeling and Form*.
35. BUBER, M., *Between Man and Man*.
36. WALKER, K., *The Physiology of Sex* and *Human Physiology* contain readable and accurate information.
37. DOSSETOR, R. F. and HENDERSON, J., *Introducing Psychology*. ADCOCK, C., *Fundamentals of Psychology*.
38. NIBLETT, W. R. (Ed.), *Moral Education in a Changing Society*.
39. The teacher cannot hope to be immediately conversant with every practical issue raised, but most school libraries provide access to the relevant information.
40. Plenty of modern novels provide situations suitable for discussion about human relationships. BARSTOW, S., *A Kind of Loving*, is an obvious example.
41. ELIOT, T. S., quoted in BANTOCK, G. H., *Education and Values*. PARRY, C. H., *The Art of Music*.
42. KEATS, J., quoted in WHITE, A., *The Hound and the Falcon*.
43. WINNICOTT, D. W., in *Youth in New Society*, Timothy Raison (Ed.).

CHAPTER 4

FROM SCHOOL TO WORK: A COUNSELLING SERVICE

CATHERINE AVENT, M.A.

*Careers Advisory Officer, London Youth Employment Service**

SEVERAL recent research projects have indicated that students in universities and other forms of continued education, as well as school-leavers making the transition from school to work, need more help and guidance than many receive at present.

Guidance on further education and careers is at present undertaken on a part-time basis by heads of secondary schools and their careers teachers and by officers of the Youth Employment Service whether administered by a local education authority or the Ministry of Labour. Careers teachers unhappily have little time or

* Catherine Avent graduated in English at Oxford. She served in the Women's Royal Naval Service as an Administrative and Education Officer from 1942 to 1947. After lecturing on careers for the Women's Employment Federation, she joined the London County Council Youth Employment Service when it was established in October 1949. She was appointed the first Careers Advisory Officer when the special section was set up for educational and vocational guidance of boys and girls preparing for a university education or professional careers.

From 1957 to 1963 Miss Avent served on the Central Advisory Council for Education (England) which produced the Crowther and Newsom Reports. She was awarded a Foreign Specialist grant by the Department of State in September 1960 in order to study counselling and guidance in the United States. She is the author of *Which Career?* and, jointly with Eleanor L. Fried, of *Starting Work*.

The views expressed in this chapter are those of the writer and not necessarily those of the Inner London Education Authority.

facilities for this task and often can do no more than direct pupils' reading and act as liaison with the Youth Employment Service principally by collating information on the pupils' abilities and aptitudes in preparation for their vocational guidance interview.

This main activity of the youth employment officer or careers adviser usually follows a programme of careers talks, possible film shows and visits to work-places. Youth employment officers advise pupils on appropriate courses of continued education, whether in school or college and, for those about to leave school, provide introductions to employers offering suitable vacancies; they follow the progress of young workers under the age of 18.

The Albemarle Report on the future development of the Youth Employment Service advocates considerable extensions of the work of this branch of the public education services; at the same time the Department of Education and Science is sponsoring short courses for careers masters and mistresses. Comprehensive schools are making provision for advice and guidance to pupils and parents faced with a wide range of educational courses, many of which have clear vocational consequences. There is, therefore, at the present time a considerable interest in the development of counselling services for young people and the advocates of extensions to the present services have been encouraged by the establishment in a few universities and colleges of education of special courses in educational guidance and counselling.

In particular, the advanced courses available in two university departments of education for teachers of 5 years' standing are a recognition of the need for the establishment of senior posts in schools to which experienced teachers can be appointed and for which special training is desirable. It has been made abundantly clear that these courses are not intended to train teachers to undertake the entire educational and vocational guidance of the pupils since this is, in the English setting, a co-operative effort between the staff of the schools and of the Youth Employment Service, but there is no doubt that the development of comprehensive schools, with their wide range of subjects, has forced authorities to consider the best way in which pupils and parents may be assisted to make suitable educational choices and to relate these to subsequent vocational opportunities. At the same time, publicity has been given to the need for industrial liaison officers and advisory services generally in the technical institutions. This has been particularly outlined in the Alexander Report on the Public Relations of Further Education and as the range of studies increases in the tertiary level of education, it is likely that there will be rapid developments in this kind of non-teaching function for some members of the staff.

THE AMERICAN PATTERN

For some years there have been suggestions that we should develop school counselling services on the American pattern but there are good reasons why this may not be appropriate in the English setting. While secondary schools here are undoubtedly becoming larger and more diverse in their range of studies and in the interests and abilities of the pupils, they are not likely to approximate to the condition of some of the large senior high schools in the U.S.A. Schools of several thousand pupils within a narrow 3 or 4 year age-range (and sometimes the only school for a large urban area) offer an enormous choice to their students. This is, of course, true in many comprehensive co-educational schools in this country but we do not ordinarily have such subjects as jewellery, cosmetology, boot repairing, report writing and speech making, for example, as formal subjects of study in the timetable. The complexities of the American credit system and the greater flexibility whereby a boy may spend half a year studying astronomy for one of his five periods a day and the next half of the year "earth science" means that over a 4-year period he can accumulate an apparently ill-assorted collection of subject-credits, not all of which may be valid for entrance to the particular colleges and universities to which he aspires on graduation from high school. The counsellor must advise him, taking into account his interests, abilities, and regular test scores, together with the requirements of the colleges and possibly his ultimate career plans. In general, the American school counsellor is much less concerned with vocational guidance because even those pupils proposing to enter what we would consider skilled crafts or technician level occupations normally train for them by means of full-time courses in 2-year colleges rather than by direct entry to employment and training on the job.

A big high school will have a team of counsellors under a director of guidance who has the status and salary of any other head of department within the school. They will be expected to sort out the students so that those in "college preparatory tracks" are persuaded to take the demanding academic courses in English, mathematics, science and languages, which will be required for entry to the better universities, while others with less academic ambition will be helped towards a reasonable spread of subjects to fit them for courses in institutions whose academic standards are less rigorous. Other pupils will only be proposing to study business education (including stenography for girls), engineering, building, catering, and all the other technical courses which in America usually involve 2 years at a junior college and in this country imply a combination of apprenticeship or other employment with attendance at a college of further education. For those with least interest in pure academic studies, the American high school may offer a range of courses in "industrial arts" and here again it is the counsellor's job to ensure that students appreciate the employment opportunities in industry or retailing or other occupations to which these courses naturally lead. So the counsellor is primarily concerned with educational choices but, at the same time, he has an important function as a general adviser to the students as a sort of "moral tutor". He will help to resolve personal problems of family or school relationships, difficulties of study or financial need, including help in obtaining a part-time job, possibly within the school as an assistant in the library, laboratory or cafeteria; in addition he concerns himself with that multitude of questions which trouble adolescents during the growing-up process. The American counsellor may find himself giving sex instruction, or marriage guidance, help on moral issues, ideas on leisure time activities, or even the kind of general advice which consists of listening to somebody's problems.

THE CAREERS TEACHER

All this is very different from the present work of the careers master in an English secondary school. His main task is one of helping pupils to acquire information about occupations, assistance when it comes to applications for college and university, and liaison with the Youth Employment Service by providing information on the pupils and making arrangements for the vocational guidance programme within the school. It is sometimes suggested that if a more intensive counselling service were developed this would take away from the class teacher and housemaster the pastoral care of his pupils which is one of the rewards and attractions of the teaching profession. This need not be so, but it is a legitimate argument against the American system which tends to place the counsellor in the position of general "trouble-shooter" to whom busy teachers refer problems which in this country they are more likely to tackle themselves.

American counsellors are often deeply involved in the school test programme. The use of psychological tests to determine abilities and aptitudes which are not always developed within the traditional school subjects is still elementary in this country. Tests have been used in, for example, Birmingham and Warrington for many years and more recently in some London schools to see what more information these reveal to help youth employment officers in assessing the vocational potentialities of boys and girls. Youth employment officers in parts of Hertfordshire and Kent have also been able to refer cases of particular difficulty for psychological testing. Many people engaged in vocational guidance believe that the expense of a comprehensive testing programme

D

would be justified by the additional information provided to those advising young people. Particular groups that come to mind are young immigrants for whom there are no school records, and pupils who appear to have better ability than their attainments indicate.

TEACHER/COUNSELLORS

A good case can be made out for the English educational system to work towards a development of half-time teacher/counsellors. These would be experienced teachers who had a particular interest in work with individual pupils, or those whose own academic background was in the social sciences or in the more obviously vocational subjects and who, therefore, had a particular interest in the world of work. If there is ever a time when teachers are not in short supply, one can envisage a situation in which experienced teachers would be seconded to attend courses, preferably of one academic year, to qualify them for teacher/counsellor appointments. As such, they would be part of the normal teaching staff of the school but freed from teaching duties for perhaps half their time in order to undertake counselling. It may be many years before enormous counselling centres on the American pattern can be built into all our secondary schools and, indeed, one might criticize these highly organized sets of offices, record systems, and information bureaux, because they can be intimidating to the 15-year-old wanting to consult a counsellor on a simple problem of choice between two alternative subjects in his course. None the less, some physical provision for a proper educational and careers guidance service should be available in each school. It is desirable, for example, for the careers literature to be readily accessible to the pupils in some place other than the careers master's form room, the science or technical teacher's laboratory or, worst of all, the headmaster's study. There are good arguments for careers literature to be in a special section of the school library but probably better ones for the provision of a separate room in which pupils can browse at leisure through the appropriate books and pamphlets and have proper facilities for taking notes at the same time.

The Newsom Report recommended that the last year of compulsory school life of pupils of average and below average academic ability should be deliberately outgoing—an initiation into the adult world of work and leisure. This implies the provision of flexible courses which might include extended extramural activities and a series of outside speakers to supplement the normal classroom activities.

The teacher/counsellor could be responsible for the organization of "Newsom courses" for pupils leaving school at the statutory age and for works-experience for those proposing to stay for an extended course, unless new legislation provides for works-experience to form part of the statutory education of boys and girls. He would organize the programme of visits to places of employment, of lectures from people representing the main occupations entered by pupils, the showing of films and filmstrips and possibly the integration with the rest of the time-table of broadcasts in careers series.

GUIDING THE UNIVERSITY ENTRANT

The teacher/counsellor would in many cases be the appropriate person to take over from the headmaster or deputy head the increasingly complex task of guiding pupils in their choice of higher and further education.

In many schools a teacher/counsellor would be the convener of an informal group composed of the heads of the various subject departments. There are schools where guidance on university entrance is entrusted to certain named teachers, very often according to the university which they themselves attended. But it is likely that a schoolmaster with a history degree from Manchester, for example, would be far better equipped to advise potential historians upon the entrance requirements for history and allied degrees in all universities than he would be able to advise boys proposing to go to Manchester to study applied sciences. Furthermore, the boy, as a rule, does not know which university he wants to go to so definitely as he knows the subjects he proposes to study, and the system of "university liaison teachers" means that he has to try to see several different masters in order to get information which instinctively he is more likely to seek from the master who teaches him his favourite or best subject. An enthusiastic young master may well enjoy having the responsibility of advising on the requirements of different universities in the subject he has himself just read, provided there is some senior member of the staff to advise parents and pupils on the other factors which influence choice of university from his experience of the extent to which pupils in that school have been successful in their applications in the past. This could well be the task of the teacher/counsellor.

Several recent research findings indicate that it is much commoner than most teachers have hitherto recognized for undergraduates to complain that they did not have sufficient advice and guidance about their higher education. Many find that they are tackling a course which is either too specialized for their interests or so different from what they had expected at school that they feel they are not likely to do justice to themselves in their final examinations. There is a particular need for advice among those students who are proceeding to universities where there is provision for transfer at the end of the first year or for the choice of major subject of study to be deferred until the completion of a foundation or general year in which three or four subjects are studied. Some pupils feel that so much emphasis has been placed in school on their getting a place in a university that they have not had sufficient advice and guidance upon the choices that may be open to them after they have embarked upon a degree course. Others have been insufficiently prepared for the difference between sixth-form work and independent study in a university.

Even more important, many undergraduates complain that they have had virtually no careers advice because it was assumed by their teachers that they should go to university with open minds or that they should concentrate all their energies upon getting into a university and not be diverted by doubts and discussion about ultimate careers. They find, therefore, on inquiry of the university appointments secretary, that they may not be studying the right subjects for a particular career or, if they had known more about the opportunities or limitations of certain careers, they might have been better advised to take a different course. Much of this comment is not made in criticism of sixth-form teachers, so much as in recognition that they have neither the time nor the facilities for giving careers advice to potential university students, because the sheer mechanism of university entry and the range of choices and particular "flavour" of courses in different universities are becoming increasingly complicated every year.

It is clear that a really effective counselling service would need several, not one, members of staff in all but the smallest single-sex schools. Teachers' interests and abilities will be given scope by the development of counselling teams, so that those attracted to the immense possibilities offered by developing "Newsom courses" can do so without feeling that they are thereby neglecting the interests of the fifth formers choosing between a sixth-form course or entry to employment or of the sixth-form students worrying about their higher education. It is still astonishing how limited is the information given to many students on the higher level courses which lead to a degree (or qualification of graduate equivalent status) which are now available in so many technical institutions. How can teachers with just a few free periods be expected to sort out which pupils should be advised to aim for diploma courses in, for example, business studies, or which should be encouraged to take employment with study for a professional qualification or a degree in one of the faculties connected with the world of commerce? More information on the variety of courses available should be readily accessible within each school.

The pupil needs, however, much more than just information and when it comes to advice on the relevance of various alternative courses to his ultimate career he should have the benefit of a discussion with a careers adviser from outside the school. The development of counselling services within the schools should lead to even greater demands on the careers officer of the Youth Employment Service.

THE YOUTH EMPLOYMENT SERVICE

This leads to a consideration of the changing role of the statutory vocational guidance and placing service for young people. Having started in 1910 with the Education (Choice of Employment) Act, the Juvenile Employment and Welfare Service, as it was originally conceived, has been undergoing a process of gradual change over the years from being primarily an employment exchange, whose officers were concerned to prevent young people from entering jobs which were harmful and generally supervising their welfare in the early years of work, until it has now become much more educationally orientated. This is a natural development from the statutory and voluntary extension of school life which has taken place during this half century. The Employment and Training Act of 1948 unfortunately retained the dual operation by providing that local education authorities had a once-for-all opportunity to choose to exercise youth employment powers and that those which did not do so at that time could never subsequently undertake this function. In these areas it is, of course, carried out by the Ministry of Labour. Although 85 per cent of the young people of the country are covered by a local authority youth employment service, it is claimed by many people that this administrative duality has no relevance in the modern educational context. It is a matter for regret in educational circles that the report on Future Development of the Youth Employment

Service recommended the retention of the dual system although it has proposed that the service should be available to young workers over 18 and failed students from tertiary education. Many people hoped for the development of counselling services without a rigid geographical division of function.

The four main functions of the Service are carried out equally by officers of local education authorities or the Ministry: the provision of careers information to young people before they leave school, giving them individual vocational guidance, placing them in suitable employment and reviewing their progress until they reach the age of 18.

Careers information is given to young people in many different ways. Most secondary schools now have quite extensive careers libraries, either as part of the main school library or in a separate place, such as a waiting or interview room, the careers master's study, sometimes his form room and, in some cases, in a senior common room, or even in a wide passage-way where pupils passing to and fro from their classes can stop to browse over the pamphlets and note the changing displays of literature on particular careers. It is sad that not all local education authorities buy for their schools the complete set of pamphlets in the official "Choice of Careers" series and criticism is justly levelled against those schools which make no attempt to keep up to date or classify the mass of material provided through the Youth Employment Service or directly from employers and professional associations. This again is due to the lack of time which most careers masters legitimately deplore.

AUDIO-VISUAL AIDS

In many schools the Youth Employment Service arranges a series of classroom sessions for the pupils in which they may listen to the regular television and sound broadcasts, and take part in discussions led by the teacher and the youth employment officer. These are intended to foster proper attitudes to the transition from school to work and sometimes include a comprehensive series of talks by people brought into the school to describe their own occupations. There is always a danger that the poor speaker on a worthwhile career may be counteracted by the glib describer of some occupation which is perhaps socially less worthy, but it is generally agreed that the opportunity to meet people actually engaged in the major occupations entered by school-leavers in the area is one of the most valuable parts of a vocational guidance programme and can even contribute to the students' general education.

There is a fairly extensive list of films which have been approved for vocational guidance purposes and there are some filmstrips to supplement this provision. If films and filmstrips are to make a worthwhile contribution to the widening horizons of young people and to extending their knowledge of occupations, it is important that they should not become isolated activities or soft options in the timetable. Careful preparation beforehand on the part of the teacher or a careers officer and follow-up afterwards to relate the topic of the film or filmstrip to the local situation and the interests of the class are essential. The Industrial Society has produced a number of excellent filmstrips to assist young people in the transition from school to work and many schools may find that even those produced primarily for use in courses for foremen and supervisors in industry can form useful introductions to general discussions on the problems of work and work situations.

CAREERS CONVENTIONS

Many schools have taken up enthusiastically the idea of careers conventions. These are particularly useful in large schools which have halls of appropriate size and facilities for entertaining the participants with suitable refreshments and ensuring that there are adequate arrangements for the setting up of any exhibition stands, photographs and demonstrations which they may bring, for car parking and for meeting parents individually or in small groups. It is not easy for small schools or those in older buildings to do this as effectively. There are differences of opinion about the appropriate stage in pupils' school lives at which they should be subjected to what, at its best, is lively and realistic careers information but, at its worst, may descend to blatant recruitment for a particular organization. Careers advisers tend to disapprove of arrangements whereby pupils are encouraged to make their choice of subjects for the fourth and fifth years of their course on the basis of information gleaned at a careers convention, since a passing fancy for electronics, for example, which has been well portrayed at a convention, may not necessarily correlate with ability in mathematics and science. On the other hand, a convention held for fifth-form pupils may be too late in that they will by then probably have decided on a broad field of work.

As with all activities of this nature, good preparation within the school is obviously necessary if pupils are to get real benefit. There is no doubt, however, that any function of this sort, which increases the mutual knowledge and understanding of the secondary schools and local industry and commerce, is to be welcomed. Some schools prefer to offer a series of more formal talks on different careers, sometimes organized to enable pupils to move from classroom to classroom in 20-minute or half-hour sessions. Here again, suitable preparation is necessary since no school can ordinarily provide for representatives of all the occupations pupils might enter and it is important that they should have their ideas enlarged rather than narrowed by this kind of activity. A nice balance has to be struck between the desire to open doors to unusual or new careers and the need to recognize that the majority of pupils will enter the traditional ones.

WORKS VISITS

One of the commonest forms of extramural activity in secondary schools is the visit to places of employment. Parties of whole forms trailing round factories and offices can degenerate into nothing more than a pleasant outing with tea at the end of the day, and employers have been known to complain that they have wasted the time of personnel officers and foremen on a group of young people not one of whom was interested in any of the occupations shown. A small party of interested boys or girls is more effective from a vocational guidance point of view but it is worth remembering that it is good for *all* young people to see different places of work as part of their general education. The extent to which industrial visits can be extended in time and depth so that pupils are actually permitted to try their hand at different operations depends on local circumstances. Works-experience is at present illegal for pupils under the statutory leaving age but a number of interesting experiments have been taking place in various parts of the country which have enabled boys and girls to get far more idea of the work involved in different occupations than they could have had from listening to lectures or even watching films or walking round a workshop. The Newsom Committee recommended experiments in outgoing courses designed to give pupils an insight into the world of work and it is likely that this sort of activity will increase markedly in the future. It is obviously of prime importance that the employers chosen to participate in any kind of extended visit or works-experience should be those recommended by the youth employment officer because they provide good training as well as good conditions for young workers.

It must be remembered, of course, that increasing numbers of school pupils have experienced a working situation during their holidays, on Saturdays, or with early morning newspaper rounds. A third of the young people who leave at the statutory age have had some kind of part-time paid employment and nearly half of those who remain in school to 16 and beyond. It is easy, therefore, to counter the argument that young people while in schools should be "protected" from the atmosphere of work-places although, of course, it must be recognized that many of the youngsters undergoing part-time employment do so in small firms and particularly in shops where there is not the likelihood of their being upset by bad language or behaviour which is obviously contrary to the standards inculcated in school. What is needed is more contact between the world of school and the world of work if young people are to be helped to make the transition from one to the other with least tension and strain.

THE SCHOOL'S ROLE

One of the weaknesses of the present counselling arrangements for English pupils has been the lack of careers activity in many grammar schools, particularly for girls. The tradition of "education for education's sake" is blamed by parents who complain that the teachers are only concerned to get the pupils into universities and colleges or that they are so preoccupied with academic considerations that they have never seriously undertaken a careers programme. Not only do the able pupils suffer because they go to university without sufficient information on the careers to which a particular degree course might lead, but those who are leaving from the fifth- and sixth-forms for employment often have much less help than pupils of comparable ability in non-selective schools. One must recognize, of course, that time is short in all these schools and that there is constant pressure as a result of the rising academic standards demanded by universities and professions. It is tempting for headmasters to feel that a significant programme of careers activity is more suitable for the less academic pupils who are not going to be confronted by external examinations but that for the potential university entrant there should be the minimum of distraction from the business of overcoming the many competitive hurdles with which these students are now faced.

While recognizing that many schools have built up close connections with particular local firms, the job of introducing a school-leaver to suitable employers is not properly one of the tasks of the careers master but rather of the careers officer from the Youth

Employment Service. Except in rare cases where, for example, a chartered accountant having no son to succeed him might offer particularly advantageous terms to an articled pupil from his own old school, a boy will normally be likely to have a wider choice of openings if he seeks employment through the Youth Employment Service. Similarly, employers have the advantage of pre-selected applicants from a wide variety of schools if they notify their vacancies to the Service rather than to particular schools known to them. The fact that the Youth Employment Service conducts a regular follow-up of young workers and its officers have more opportunity than teachers for visiting employers to discuss training and recruitment and also to get "the feel of the firm" provides a regular feed-back of information with which the officers can advise succeeding generations of school-leavers.

Among many rival suggestions for improving the careers guidance available in schools and, in particular, for preparing for the raising of the school-leaving age, one might suggest something on the lines of the New York High School Programme. In this the counsellors, who are full-time officials of the State Employment Service, spend 4 days of each week during term in schools giving information and guidance on employment, advice on continued full-time education being the prerogative of the school counsellor who is, of course, a member of the school staff. On Fridays all the employment counsellors are gathered together in the employment office for conferences, research work, visiting employers and so on. They return to the office during the school holidays and are thus available to help students and young workers at times when the school teacher/counsellors are themselves on vacation. The school counsellors are established teachers who have undertaken a course, usually for a Master's degree, and are then appointed as full-time staff of the counselling centre within the school. Their task is to give educational guidance and advice on personal problems, and they themselves have excellent prospects to progress to become director of guidance or head counsellor within the school, or as an administrator of guidance services within the education office of the authority. Equally, they are eligible for promotion to be headmasters or educational administrators because they have not been divorced from the normal teaching role in which they supplement their individual counselling duties with classroom work on the teaching of occupations. There is no doubt that some such parallel development in this country would be of great advantage to young people if ever there were a time when teachers and youth employment officers were sufficiently numerous to make this practicable.

THE FUTURE

The Youth Employment Service needs a vast expansion in order to provide more intensive work in the schools and it has high hopes of increasing staff as a result of the Albemarle Report. Ultimately there may be legislation requiring every local education authority to operate a careers advisory service equipped to assist men and women over the age of 18 whose need for educational and vocational guidance, as well as merely a new job, may be much greater in future if the economists' predictions are fulfilled and most adults have to have three or four different occupations in a working life.

One obvious development which many would welcome would be joint training courses for teachers and careers advisers. This would be preferable to the suggestion of joint counselling courses for experienced teachers and advisers since a dual initial qualification would enable men and women to transfer at different stages in their careers from the teaching to the advisory role. They would each have the same promotion prospects within the schools and in administration, the inspectorate, teacher training and so on. The Department of Education and Science is encouraging work-experience schemes for student teachers and for some experienced members of school staffs. (Teachers will welcome this development while at the same time resisting the spread of the curious myth that teachers are "ignorant of life", and inhabit a cloistered world set apart from their fellow men and women!) Comparable secondments would be valuable for careers advisers to enable them to spend a few weeks, either teaching or in personnel offices, attached to university appointments boards or Ministry of Labour employment exchanges. In this way there would be greater cross-fertilization of ideas and techniques, and progress made towards the ideal system of complete mutual confidence and co-operation between the teacher/counsellors in the schools and the careers advisers outside, which is the ultimate goal of all who hope to see better help given to young people in the transition from education to employment.

CHAPTER 5

THE PROFESSIONAL SOCIAL WORKER

NANCY HAZEL, B.A.

Lecturer in Applied Social Studies, Nottingham University*

THE EMERGENCE OF A PROFESSION

It is more confusing to talk about social work than it is to talk about teaching, because social work is only just emerging as a recognized profession. In a sense, social work is as old as charity, but professional social work in its modern form has only grown up during the last hundred years and its recognition as part of the statutory social services followed the Second World War. Many people thought that the coming of the welfare state marked the end of the "charitable" tradition of social work, but today voluntary social work flourishes in many forms and it is possible that the conscious desire to help others may be more widespread than at any other period. Certainly the tremendous response of young people to such movements as International Voluntary Service or Community Service Volunteers is a genuine charitable impulse and the ready financial response to appeals such as Oxfam seems to show that this feeling spans the generations.

* Nancy Hazel worked with France Combattante and the Control Commission for Germany, took the first Child Service Course at Birmingham University, and joined the newly formed Children's Department of East Sussex. In 1961 she started the first 2-year Child Care course at Birmingham College of Commerce, and in 1965 was appointed Lecturer in Applied Social Studies, Nottingham University.

Probably freedom from want and squalor, together with improved educational opportunities, liberates energy which may be directed towards altruistic goals.

This energy is the raw material of the newest specialism in professional social work—*community work*. So far, few universities or colleges offer this type of training, but it is to be expected that the awareness of need for a service of this kind, both in the United Kingdom (particularly in areas of urban renewal or twilight zones) and in the newly developing countries, will lead to the provision of courses. In this field the "salaried expert", who may in present-day conditions be quite untrained and rather light on expertise, collaborates with every kind of voluntary worker. This may mean helping the half-a-dozen isolated mothers who come together to plan a discussion group (no one is paid, no official organization is involved), or the same people, planning a play group—where it may be necessary to notify the Medical Officer of Health and where more complicated knowledge and facilities are needed; or it may mean encouraging and co-ordinating the efforts of established voluntary bodies (such as the Red Cross), whose unpaid workers are anxious to start such activities as clubs for old or handicapped people—involving considerable organization and accommodation. It is important to distinguish between the unpaid and untrained voluntary worker—whose contribution may be as little as selling flags in the street once a year or as much as befriending a difficult discharged prisoner—and the salaried professional social worker employed by a voluntary body. Each role makes different demands on time and skill; all are valuable, but the focus of this chapter will be on professional, rather than voluntary, social work.

Thus the main function of community work is an enabling one, building on the strengths which are already there, but it sometimes involves taking the initiative and the role of leader. In many localities work of this kind is undertaken by councils of social service. Sometimes community work will start by attempting to gain the confidence and mobilizing the resources of communities with a reputation for difficult and anti-social behaviour, and here the worker may have to face the problem of hostility from the local "respectable" elements. In other instances, as the encouragement of community feeling leads to increased social interaction among the "respectable" and encouraged groups, so the isolation of the delinquent or anti-social groups may be perpetuated by the open disdain of the "respectable" elements which is likely to evoke further non-conformity.[1] To understand the way a community defends itself against uncomfortable members and to prevent the escalating effects of such situations is also a part of the community worker's skill.

Community work is concerned with the way groups of people behave and interact within a larger community; *group work*, the next specialism of social work, has, as its material, individuals interacting within groups small enough for them to meet face to face. Again, not all universities and colleges which offer social work training courses offer facilities for group work, but the number of such courses is increasing from year to year.

Social group work implies knowledge and understanding of the way in which individuals create the group and the group influences the individual members. Such pressures are extremely powerful—as any teacher knows. This knowledge and understanding may be used in various ways. For example, it may be used in youth clubs to create a milieu in which the timid outsider may be helped to feel accepted and confident, or the noisy barracker learn to take responsibility. It may be used in organizations for handicapped people of all kinds to help them to help each other in facing the realities of their future and overcoming their anxieties or despair. Finally, it may be used in the area where social work and therapy meet—to help people in their efforts to resolve or come to terms with pervasive personality problems, such as may be found in deprived children, probationers, offenders in prison or mental hospital patients. Obviously these categories overlap—physically handicapped people may have deep personality problems and probationers may be normal, mature people—

but the focus of work will differ from one group to another. In England surprisingly little use has been made so far of this technique to help parents of children whose difficulties become apparent in the school setting. Many voluntary bodies are engaged in work with groups and the role of leader is filled by a wide range of people—ranging from the part-time, unpaid and untrained youth leader to the fully trained and experienced salaried social worker, but in both the statutory and voluntary services far too few fully trained group workers are as yet available.

Many of the people who are now experimenting with groups started as social caseworkers, and it is the members of this branch of the profession who are probably most easily identified by the public as "social workers". *Social casework* is concerned with the one-to-one interaction between a professional worker and a person with a problem. This interaction may range from the simple giving of information to a joint exploration of areas of intense feeling. Like group and community work, it is supportive, enabling and non-directive. This branch of work forms the core of all social work training courses. Casework is the oldest branch of social work and a change of attitude and method has taken place during the last few years. From a more or less exclusive pre-occupation with the one-to-one interview, which enabled a considerable degree of expertise to be developed, the focus has come to include the family as a whole. This has called for the development of skill in multiple interviewing and blurred the previous sharp boundary between casework and group work. Thus the profession as it exists today shows a continuum from work with communities to work with the individual.

THE SCHOOL AND THE SOCIAL CASEWORKERS

Obviously social work touches the life of the school at many points. The school is part of the community and a potent force in forming and changing attitudes. The school is linked in various ways to innumerable groups in which both staff and children participate in many ways, and social caseworkers will often be in contact with the children, their families and the school itself. All heads of schools have many meetings with social workers, but it is difficult to assess how often the other teachers meet the social workers to discuss problems common to both of them; certainly both sides often harbour suspicions that the other "does not really understand". The social work role of the school varies too—to a headmaster this may mean visiting the family of every child in the school, or such visiting may be seen as inappropriate for teachers. Special counselling appointments are rare. Most schools make strenuous efforts to maintain good relationships with parents either by interviews at the school, by parent–teacher associations or by home visiting—but Marsden and Jackson in their study of grammar school children from working class homes[2] describe the difficulties which working class parents encountered in communicating with educational institutions, and Douglas, studying all children born during one week in March 1956,[3] states that "the parents who are most interested in their children's education come predominantly from the middle classes, and those who are least interested from the working classes". It is clear, too, that teachers have neither the time nor the professional knowledge and skills to carry out intensive social casework, yet, at the same time, the need for fuller social work participation by teachers is urgent.

Who, then, are the social caseworkers and what do they do? Firstly, there are a great many of them. Traditionally, in England, a need for help is identified and a service—either voluntary or State—is set up to meet it. Each service then tends to become independent and proud of its achievements. As no one person or body of persons exists to perform the function of "overlord", the proliferation of services continues and learning about their functions and administration takes up a substantial part of all social work training programmes. (A list of all the statutory and voluntary agencies which are available is concisely set out in the Family Welfare Association's publications, *The Annual Charities Register and Digest* and *Guide to the Social Services*.)

The problem of overlapping and waste of expensive resources is obvious. In 1950 an important circular was issued jointly by the Home Office, the Ministry of Health and the Ministry of Education. Under the title *Children Neglected or Ill-treated in their Own Homes* attention was drawn to the necessity of "considering the needs of the family as a whole if effective action is to be taken to deal with child neglect". Many co-ordination committees and conferences were set up as a result of the recommendations contained in this circular and unnecessary duplication of visiting has certainly been reduced, but many of the problems of establishing mutual understanding between workers trained in different disciplines and with different ideas as to what the needs of problem families really are, remain unsolved. The Government White Paper, *The Child, the Family and the Young Offender* (Cmnd. 2742), which appeared in 1965, points the way to a family service, but deep differences of attitude and technique will remain as long as some social workers are totally untrained, some inadequately trained and some highly trained. Even those social workers who actually visit the schools are numerous and extremely varied in their level of skill and professional background. In addition, difficulties may arise due to the complexity of the relationships between voluntary and statutory bodies.

I. VOLUNTARY ORGANIZATIONS

1. *The National Society for the Prevention of Cruelty to Children's* inspector is one of the doyens of social work—his origins go back to the last quarter of the nineteenth century and he has performed the socially approved role of rescuer ever since. He is approved both by the very large number of people whose subscriptions and legacies help to finance the Society and by the families at risk which he visits—for example, Pauline Morris in her study of prisoners' families, describes how wives looked on the "cruelty man" as a particularly benevolent and helpful figure.[4] He is authorized by law to bring children before a juvenile court in

cases of neglect or cruelty and he is also empowered to bring a prosecution against the parents in the adult court. His Society does not, however, itself provide care for the children it removes—this is usually provided by the local authority children's departments or the voluntary children's societies—nor is the Society wholly financed from private funds, since it receives substantial grants from the local authorities. In the last few years the way in which the inspector carries out his duties has changed considerably. He no longer advertises himself as setting out to punish "bad" parents and "save" their children, but, in conjunction with women workers now being appointed, as trying to help and befriend families with children who are in trouble of almost any kind.

It is difficult to generalize about the degree of skill and the techniques employed by N.S.P.C.C. inspectors. In 1960 the report of the Ingleby Committee on Children and Young Persons stated that "few of the inspectors or visitors are qualified social workers" and recommended that authority to initiate proceedings should be confined to the police or local authority (para. 87). This recommendation has not been implemented but two developments have taken place.

(a) The N.S.P.C.C. has agreed to consult the children's officer whenever court action is contemplated, so that a careful plan for the child's future can be worked out together on a basis of shared information, although the society can still take independent action if it feels this to be in the interests of the child.

(b) The length of training provided by the N.S.P.C.C. for newly recruited inspectors and women visitors has been extended from 6 months to 1 year and a steady trickle of serving inspectors are being seconded to the 2-year courses leading to the national Certificate in Social Work, and other relevant courses. The prevention of cruelty to children is always an issue which rouses strong feelings and the natural desire to "save" the unhappy child. We are, however, only just beginning to understand that physical ill-treatment may, in fact, hurt a child less than the loss of its family and known environment, and accurate knowledge of the kind of parents who ill-treat their children is still lacking. In this kind of work it is particularly easy to do harm with the best of good intentions and there is no substitute for knowledge and the unremitting search for understanding.

Thus the work of the N.S.P.C.C. remains as important as it has ever been, but different and still changing. How will it fit into a future family service which can already (through children's departments) give assistance in cash and kind, care for children where this is appropriate, and provide a casework service to the family as a whole? It is the typical problem facing so many old-established charitable organizations—to be flexible enough to create a new and different role in response to changing needs.

2. *The moral welfare worker* is likely to visit schools in connection with girls who may be pregnant or "in moral danger". Like the N.S.P.C.C. inspectors, she was one of the early social workers to appear, and similarly her role today is less clear-cut than it used to be. Her work consists mainly of helping mothers with illegitimate babies, a little matrimonial work, a little general welfare work with families, and some educational work on matters of morals and sex.[5] Work with young girls is being increasingly taken over by children's departments who are able to provide a family casework service and accommodation in children's homes or hostels. For the majority of unmarried mothers with whom she is in touch, the moral welfare worker provides counselling and practical help, accommodation in mother and baby homes where appropriate, and an adoption-placing service if this is needed. Moral welfare is thus a relatively specialized activity.

Most moral welfare workers are employed by local or diocesan committees under the auspices of the Church of England and are advised by a Committee of the Board for Social Responsibility of the Church Assembly. They are thus working as members of the Church of England and are paid from voluntary funds, although they normally have substantial grants from the local authority. There are a few workers in this field from other denominations and a few local authorities employ their own workers. Training for moral welfare workers, residential as well as fieldworkers, is provided on a Christian non-denominational basis at Josephine Butler House in Liverpool (founded in 1920). Candidates, aged over 23, take a 2-year course, but may include an additional year to obtain the Social Science Certificate at the University of Liverpool. There is a shorter course for older women. Moral welfare workers have always been recognized as trained caseworkers, but, as other branches of social work have grown in importance and opportunities for professional training at universities and colleges have increased, moral welfare has been left with a limited choice of recruits, mainly older and less academic women. It is also left with the problem of defining its own future role—if the State provides a family service and there are other non-denominational sources for matrimonial counselling, in what way should Christian social work make its distinctive contribution?

3. *Children's societies*. During the nineteenth century a number of societies with a denominational religious basis were set up to help the large numbers of homeless and orphaned children. These well-known societies continue their work today and, with the addition of the much more recent National Association for Mental Health, co-operate with each other through the National Council of Associated Children's Homes. The present membership of the Council is:

Dr. Barnardo's Homes
The Catholic Child Welfare Society
The Church of England Children's Society
The Invalid Children's Aid Society
The National Association for Mental Health
The National Children's Home
The Norwood Joint Committee for the Welfare of Jewish Children
The Salvation Army

The Shaftesbury Homes and *Arethusa* Training Ship
The Shaftesbury Society

There are, of course, many smaller societies and homes.

The traditional core of the work of these societies has been providing residential accommodation for children in need, but round this there has grown up a network of services for fostering and adoption. Some of the residential establishments provide their own schooling, but most children in the care of voluntary homes will attend local schools. Few of them will now be orphans; many will be illegitimate, many will be coloured. On the whole, they will be children who are separated from their families for a long time; shorter breaks and emergencies tend to be dealt with by the local children's departments. As the needs of children for individual care have become better understood, and as child destitution apart from their parents no longer exists as a social problem, so the voluntary societies have been faced with the challenge of adapting their resources to meet changing needs. Some societies have turned their resources to schemes for rehabilitating the family as a whole (Barnardo's, Middlemore Homes); others have concentrated on specialized approaches to specific handicaps—for example, the Invalid Children's Aid Society's work for autistic children. It is not an easy task for these old societies to leave their traditional role and think afresh, but they are certainly aware of the challenge.

4. *The Family Service Unit* (F.S.U.). In the case of the N.S.P.C.C. inspector, the moral welfare worker and the voluntary children's homes, we have seen old-established organizations, who led the way in the past, whose work has been largely taken over by the State and who are now searching for ways in which to adapt and modify themselves to meet the changing needs of a new kind of society. In the case of the F.S.U. we can see a fairly new organization which now plays a remarkably important part in forming professional opinion and influencing the making of policy.

F.S.U.s were formed in 1947 to continue and broaden the extensive casework service for problem families which had been started during the war by pacifist service units in Liverpool, Manchester and London. These original units set out to offer help to the "hopeless" cases whom existing services had abandoned. In these multi-problem families repeated visiting, advice and warnings had eventually produced either apathy or hostile, anti-social behaviour. The aims of the F.S.U. were:

(a) to provide a service undertaking intensive and comprehensive welfare work among families unable to maintain proper standards of home and child care without special assistance. It places the service at the disposal of other departments and bodies to be used by them on particular cases needing specialized treatment;

(b) to develop a preventive service so that disintegration may be averted by timely help;

(c) to conduct a comprehensive research project to study the causes which lead to the disintegration of family life.

The early days of the units set the tone for all subsequent development:

> Conscious of their inexperience, they began by offering the humblest services and attempting to find a sound basis for their relationship to the families. . . . Cleaning, decorating, removing, repairing and disinfesting were the first forms of service and on this basis the rest was built. Friendship was made the foundation of the work.

In the 6th Annual Report (for 1953–4) this has become a professional relationship but does not lose its distinctive flavour:

> although F.S.U. workers are inevitably involved in a great variety of very practical and concrete activities, these activities are meaningful and effective only within the medium of the relationship between the worker and the members of the family, which is a relationship of warmth and genuine concern. . . . The very essence of the service is in this relationship. Essentially it is the human response of one person to another in need; a response, however, which must be disciplined if it is to meet the needs of the family effectively. Hence the necessity for the most careful selection of workers and the importance of adequate training and skilled supervision. [6]

Since 1954 the F.S.U. has provided practical training for a substantial number of the students on the post-credential professional training courses and is now extending this service to students from the non-university professional courses. Their research project made a major contribution to the literature when, in 1963, A. F. Philp published *Family Failure*, a study of 129 families with multiple problems. Finally, the emphasis on family casework in local authority health, welfare and children's departments owes much to the F.S.U., whose influence can also clearly be seen in the shift of government policy towards expanding preventive casework services.

An interesting project, using an approach similar to that of the F.S.U., is recorded in *The Canford Families* (Sociological Review Monograph No. 6, Keele, 1962). Here an agency was set up for an experimental period of 5 years, financed by charitable trusts, to offer a preventive group work and casework service to families with children at school whose behaviour was causing concern. The team sought to help the family as a unit and sixteen families were helped and studied intensively for periods varying from 16 to 27 months. This study makes very clear the interrelatedness of family problems—for example, the children's progress may be linked with the state of the marital relationship or the father's performance of his role. Emphasis is laid on the importance of early contact with families at risk, and on the fact that these families have potentiality to function better and to live more happily.

5. *The Family Welfare Association* and *the Family Discussion Bureau*. It is not only newly created voluntary agencies which may take the lead in professional thinking—one of the oldest agencies of all, the Family Welfare Association, has made contributions of great current importance.

The present-day Family Welfare Association is the descendant of the London Charity Organization Society, founded in 1869. It functions as a family casework agency, comparable to the personal service committees of many councils of social service, and makes a major contribution to the training of students. But the unique part which it has played in the recent social work scene is as instigator or participator in experiments which have been carefully recorded and published. The best-known project is the Family Discussion Bureau. This originated as a small pilot unit set up in 1948, with the support of the Tavistock Institute of Human Relations, to try and discover how far social workers could offer help with marital difficulties. Bureau workers (including both caseworkers and psychiatrists who work together as a team) have concentrated on the task of evolving the special casework skills they felt were required for therapeutic work and applying them to meet the needs of the married couples experiencing serious difficulties referred to them by other casework organizations and citizens' advice bureaux. The Bureau has also carried on training schemes for general practitioners, health visitors and social workers and produced a series of publications which have been widely used in the training of students. [7] In this way the influence of this relatively small project has been extremely far-reaching.

Another interesting project, this time to test out the possibilities of several bodies working together as a unit in one area, was started in 1963 when the Family Welfare Association, the Family Service Units and the Invalid Children's Aid Association, with the financial support of the London parochial charities, established the Family Centre of Hackney and Stoke Newington. Each of the three bodies takes part in the staffing and management of the centre, which provides within one administrative unit casework services elsewhere provided by the three organizations separately. It will operate for an initial experimental period of 5 years and it is hoped that in this time the bodies concerned will be able to assess the casework needs of the area and see what benefits come from the combined operation.

Finally, before turning to the statutory services, two other voluntary organizations are of great importance to the families of children in schools, although their representatives are not professional social workers and are unlikely to be in direct contact with the school itself.

6. *Marriage Guidance Councils* are voluntary bodies both in the sense that they are non-statutory (although grant-aided) but also because the counsellors are volunteers. The original Marriage Guidance Council was formed in London in 1938, but its early development was inevitably interrupted by the war, and it was not until 1945 that the first steps were taken towards providing a training for lay counsellors. Outside London, similar activity had been taking place, so that by April 1946 there were the beginnings of local marriage guidance councils in many places. In 1947 the National Marriage Guidance Council was set up to act as a co-ordinating body and to carry the responsibility for selection and training of volunteers. The 122 local councils are self-governing within a framework of principles which have been agreed by all and provide the actual service, which is in part educational and in part remedial. The councils are undenominational in both work and membership, but the Roman Catholic Church has its own Marriage Advisory Council based on its own beliefs and teaching.

Perhaps the outstanding characteristic of the Council is the rigorous demands it makes on the volunteer counsellors. Firstly, the elaborate and searching selection procedure eliminates many of the original applicants. Those who are accepted are expected to undergo in their own time a training which makes substantial intellectual and emotional demands. Marriage counselling is difficult because it deals with a fundamental human relationship. It is also difficult because it requires the counsellor to refrain from giving advice, imposing a solution or apportioning blame. The counsellor listens to the clients' stories in a friendly, unhurried atmosphere, helping them to face up to their feelings and attitudes, to appreciate their partners' needs as well as their own and to work their way through to decisions acceptable to themselves. The counsellor must be aware, too, of the boundaries of his own competence, the points at which he needs to involve the appropriate consultant, medical, psychiatric, legal or spiritual, and the points where his own feelings or prejudices begin to intrude. Here the work of marriage guidance has done much to develop techniques of consultation and case discussion appropriate to such extremely intimate and confidential matters.

7. *The Family Planning Association* (F.P.A.) started just over 40 years ago when a few pioneering women of great courage and integrity started birth control clinics mainly to help poor women with large families. It still relies upon 3000 voluntary workers, mainly women, but employs doctors and nurses who are usually paid professional rates. It does not provide a domiciliary service. Poor women still have large families and their children are smaller and lighter, do less well at school and are more frequently delinquent than those from smaller families. It is, however, questionable how well the F.P.A. meets their needs.

In 1959 the Association set up a working party under the chairmanship of Professor Francois Lafitte to review the position and in 1963 a report was produced. The working party agreed that birth control was now widely, but not universally, approved in Britain, that approval was greater among the higher social classes than the lower but was increasing in all classes. In the great majority of cases the preference is for the husband to take the precautions. Only a small minority get professional advice about birth control.

In 1961 only 37 local health authorities provided birth control clinics, and these only served women who needed contraceptive advice on medical grounds. At the same time 336 clinics were provided by the F.P.A. In these clinics the focus was predominantly on female methods, and relatively few clients were the wives of unskilled manual workers. The working party felt convinced that the National Health Service must, in the long run, provide the public with the services at present offered by the F.P.A., but recommended, meanwhile, certain organizational changes to enable the F.P.A. to become the main focus of interest for all with expert knowledge of the problems associated with human fertility regulation and the means of effecting it, and that greater stress should be laid on the need to offer advice on all aspects and methods of family planning for both men and women, allowing time for questions and discussion and a personal choice of method.

So the F.P.A., founded to help poor women, but in fact helping largely middle class women and faced with an eventual take-over by the State, has already taken steps towards the formulation of a new and constructive future role. And now an independent charity, Brook Advisory Centres Ltd., is planning to set up a chain of eighteen regional clinics to advise the young and un-married on birth control. The first clinic was started in London in 1963, but there is considerable public opposition to the project. It has, however, always been the function of voluntary organiza-tions to test out new and controversial ideas.

8. *"Self-help" organizations.* In the past voluntary bodies have mainly grown out of the combined endeavour of a number of people who have felt concern about the plight of others and have formed an organization to meet the needs of which they had become aware. Today, a number of organizations spring from the enterprise of the "afflicted" group itself, bringing together interested people to press for improvements. Such groups are the National Society for Mentally Handicapped Children or the Muscular Dystrophy Group. The role of these organizations seems to be twofold:

(a) to act as a pressure group demanding reform;
(b) by social interaction to reassure and help the members themselves.

It is predictable that with improved education such self-help is likely to increase.

Such a rapid sampling of the voluntary social services which affect the lives of children at school does not do justice to this distinctive sector of British culture, but the part which this voluntary contribution plays can only be distinguished in the context of the statutory services which, in a welfare state, are theoretically designed to meet the requirements of anyone in need, and are not entitled (as the voluntary services may legitimately do) to choose their clients. The way in which clients and services do in fact "choose" each other is discussed in connection with the Smith family in the following chapter.

II. THE SOCIAL CASEWORKER
IN THE STATUTORY SERVICES

1. *The probation officer* will be a fairly frequent visitor as in most schools some children indulge in behaviour which is against the law—and are found out. (The "dark number" who are not found out has probably included most of us.) The probation officer, usually a man for boys or a woman for girls, may be undertaking voluntary supervision of a child whose behaviour gives cause for anxiety, or he may be carrying out an inquiry where the child is old enough to have been charged with an offence* and is about to appear before the juvenile court, or he may be carrying out the instructions of the court where the child has been found guilty and placed on probation, or found to be "in need of care, protection or control" and placed under his supervision. In simple terms, he is either trying to find out what is wrong or trying to help the child to get on better.

To find out what is wrong, he needs all the help the school can give. What is the child's level of attainment? Does he seem to be working at full stretch or is he failing to learn? Where are the areas of stress or failure? Is he a popular child, a bully, a withdrawn, isolated child? How does he get on with adults? How easily can the school and parents talk to each other?

The probation officer has much help to offer the teacher too. He understands the way of life of the neighbourhood. He knows about the overcrowded conditions at home or the quarrels between the parents or the financial troubles which may distract the child's thoughts. He can see where a stepchild is picked on or

---

* Defined as over 10 years by the Children and Young Persons Act, 1963, Section 16 (1).

the youngest-but-one pushed out of favour by the last-born. He knows if the parents allow the child freedom and opportunity to develop his own interests or if they stifle him with do's and don'ts in their anxiety to produce a perfect and successful child; if they provide books and intellectual stimulation or consider education to be something foreign, incomprehensible and a hindrance to doing something more useful.

Of course, when a child appears before a juvenile court, the school provides a report for the magistrates to read, but teachers do not often attend the court themselves and the probation officer is there to bridge the gap between court and school. Perhaps it would help if teachers were able to attend more often—particularly the person who really knows the child, as a headmaster's report tends to be a rather brief and formal document. The importance of a good understanding between the court and the school is paramount, as the court has the power to send the child away from both his home and his school. The probation officer may be expected to understand the home situation and it is the function of the school to make clear where the child's difficulties lie and exactly what help it can or cannot offer. What the court needs is an objective analysis, not value judgements such as "a good boy" or "a bad influence".

2. *The child care officer* will be the next most frequent visitor (the title "children's officer" is only given to the chief officer of the children's department) and his work often overlaps that of the probation officer. By the Children and Young Persons Act, 1963, he was given the duty to "promote the welfare of children by diminishing the need to receive children into or keep them in care . . . or to bring children before a juvenile court". He is also specifically charged with investigating behaviour which appears to be beyond the parent's control, and allegations of cruelty and neglect. It is therefore essential for him to receive from the teacher information about children who are beginning to show signs of unhappy or anti-social behaviour. Unless he receives this early warning, he cannot carry out his preventive role.

The child care officer has an additional set of duties which differ from those of the probation officer. Where a child, for any reason, can no longer live with his own parents, it is the child care officer's duty to make the necessary arrangements for his care, to watch over his present welfare and to plan for his future. Usually the future will hold an eventual return to his own parents, but some children may remain in care until they are grown up. For children in care the most satisfactory provision is often a foster home, where the children are able to live in an ordinary family group in an ordinary community, but this is not an easy way of living for any of the people concerned. It is hard for a family to absorb outsiders, it is hard, too, for an "outsider" to become "one of us"—and the "outsider's" parents may not be easy to accept and make welcome. Nevertheless, fostering at its best is extremely successful both for the children and for the foster parents, but help and understanding is needed from both the social worker and the school. For example, a foster child's name is different from that of its foster parents; this *must* be recognized and accepted, not muddled or glossed over as if it were something shameful or mysterious. A foster child is always very quick to feel different and inferior. And the foster parents naturally prefer to be given their own name, not that of the child's parents! Even foster homes which are privately arranged *must* be supervised by the child care officer.

Other children may live in homes, either large or small, with professional houseparents, and come to school in a group. Children in homes almost always feel "different", although they may be helped successfully to come to terms with this feeling and with the realities of their situation.

With children in care, the child care officer, the foster parents and the houseparents all need help from the school. They have not had the opportunity to watch the growth and development of their children from the beginning, as parents are able to do, and they need all the information they can get to help them to understand and plan to meet the children's needs.

E

Lastly, the child care officer is concerned with adoptions. Children may be placed for adoption by the children's department, by adoption societies or privately, but *all*** adoptions are supervised by the child care officer during the probationary period before the final order is made. Most children placed for adoption are babies, but older foster children are sometimes adopted by their foster parents and mothers often adopt their own child in order to make a new husband into the child's legal father.

So, like the probation officer, the child care officer may be instrumental in removing the child from his home—either by means of an order made by the juvenile court because the child is held to be "in need of care, protection or control", or, at the request of the parents or with their agreement, because they are "prevented" from caring for him (Children Act, 1948, Section 1) or in order to place him for adoption. It is a heavy responsibility.

3. *The psychiatric social worker* from the child guidance clinic is the third visitor often seen at the school. A child showing disturbed behaviour may be referred to the clinic by the school itself, by the parents or by other people or agencies, often the family doctor. The child and his mother, and sometimes the father and other family members, will attend the clinic regularly where treatment will be carried out by the team of psychiatrist, educational psychologist and psychiatric social worker. Of course, any member of the team may contact the school, and the educational psychologist will often do so, but it is the psychiatric social worker who will be most concerned with the child's social environment, and with the school in this sense. Like the probation officer and the child care officer, he will have built up a picture of the child in his family and he will need to complete this study by seeing how the child relates to the school environment. For some children difficulties arise both at home and at school; others are happy at home but find school difficult; for others, school may be a welcome refuge from the stresses of home. The psychiatric social worker has the same need for full and objective information as the other

* In a few areas this supervision is still carried out by health visitors.

social workers and will, like them, want to work out a joint treatment plan. He also may, together with the other members of the clinic team, arrange for a child to leave his home if it is decided that this is a maladjusted child whose needs will best be met by a period in a residential school or by treatment in hospital.

4. *The medical social worker* (formerly known as almoner) is another social worker who will be involved in the lives of many children and their parents, but will not very often visit the school. The medical social worker is usually based on a hospital and it is her function to help patients and their families to overcome the personal and social difficulties and stresses which so frequently accompany and follow illness. Her help to children and their families can be seen to be particularly important in view of John Bowlby's investigations[8] of the dangers of separating children from their parents, particularly by hospitalization, where separation is accompanied by pain, fear and a totally strange kind of environment. The medical social worker can do much to keep the bond between the child and his family alive and to help both sides to understand and come to terms with what is often a terrifying and bewildering experience.

5. *The education welfare officer* has been left until the last, although he visits the school more often than the probation officer, the child care officer, or the psychiatric social worker, and, like the teachers, is an employee of the local education committee. The four kinds of social worker which have been described may not always do their work very effectively, but they have a fairly clear idea of the function which they are attempting to perform and the techniques of social casework which they are trying to use can be identified. It is difficult to make a clear statement about the role of the education welfare officer. His name has been changed from school attendance to education welfare officer, but in some authorities his time is still mainly taken up by routine checks on absence, by arranging for offending parents to receive a committee warning, and by initiating prosecutions. Where he attempts to help parents his techniques are usually exhortation,

explanation or rebuke, and with children encouragement, exhortation or rebuke. Many authorities are making strenuous efforts to re-think and reorganize this service on more sophisticated social work lines, and many education welfare officers are in fact extremely sensitive and effective social workers. But there is no social work qualification or training* required for these posts, and consequently there is a great variation in the level of skill and the social work goals which are envisaged.

Beyond the services which touch the child in the school lie a whole range of health and welfare services to which his family may turn for help. In particular, difficulties arising from mental illness or subnormality will be the concern of the mental welfare officer and troubles due to physical infirmity or handicap will be dealt with by the social welfare officer. For the family as whole, the health visitor is available and she will be in contact with all mothers of very small children.

Like the voluntary services, the statutory services have grown up over the years and they, too, face the task of reorganization, both in order to provide a more effective service to families and to avoid the wasteful and overlapping use of scarce resources.

REFERENCES

1. SPENCER, J., *Stress and Release on an Urban Estate*, Tavistock, 1964.
2. MARSDEN, D. and JACKSON, B., *Education and the Working Class*, Routledge, 1962.
3. DOUGLAS, J. W. B., *The Home and the School*, McGibbon & Kee, 1964.
4. MORRIS, P., *Prisoners and their Families*, Allen & Unwin, 1965.
5. PENELOPE HALL, M. and HOWES, I. V., *The Church in Social Work*, Routledge, 1965.
6. PHILP, A. and TIMMS, N., *The Problem of the Problem Family*, F.S.U., 1962.
7. Publications of the Family Discussion Bureau: *Social Casework in Marital Problems*, Tavistock, 1955; *Marriage: studies in emotional conflict and growth*, Methuen, 1960; *The Marital Relationship as a Focus for Casework*, Codicote Press, 1962; *Shared Fantasy in Marital Problems*, Codicote Press, 1965.
8. BOWLBY, J., *Child Care and the Growth of Love*, Pelican, 1965 ed.

* The Certificate in Education Welfare requires students to demonstrate in writing some knowledge of social work and of the social services, but does not require any supervised casework or group work practice.

CHAPTER 6

THE TASK OF SOCIAL WORK

NANCY HAZEL, B.A.

THE CLIENT—THE SMITH FAMILY

Now let us look at a family, which might be real but is not. There are a great many families which closely resemble this one; they have not committed any serious offences so they have never appeared in court and have therefore little contact with probation officers. No one is currently in hospital so that neither the medical social worker nor the psychiatric social worker (or the mental welfare officer) is in touch with them, but of course these workers easily might already have been involved.

Mr. Smith is aged 38. He went to an all-age school and then worked as a labourer. He has a slight back lesion due to an industrial injury, but received no compensation—Mr. Smith thinks the decision was unfair, and feels "unmanly" doing light work. He is frequently out of a job, usually because he feels "picked on" and answers back or walks out. At the pub he regains his self-esteem by buying drinks—and drinks to fortify himself against returning home to face his wife. He has no contact with his family of origin—they are ashamed of him. Some people would call him a malingerer, a drunkard and a bad father, and he is aware of this.

Mrs. Smith is aged 35. She was an illegitimate child, brought up by her maternal grandmother. Her mother died of tuberculosis. The family were very poor and Mrs. Smith has difficulty with reading and writing. Her only relative is the grandmother, who is very old. Mrs. Smith is not a "good manager" and the house is dirty and untidy. She knows what the neighbours think about her.

The children of the family are: Jean, aged 15, George, aged 12, Arthur, aged 10, Peter, aged 9, Timmy, aged 4, Mary, aged 4 weeks.

The family live in a three-bedroomed council house.

Mr. and Mrs. Smith married when they realized that Mrs. Smith was pregnant with Jean, so they did not save up any money for their future home. Shortly after Jean's birth, Mrs. Smith spent a period in a sanatorium and her mother looked after Jean. Mr. Smith was in hospital for a period following his accident after Peter was born, and after that there was one stillborn child.

Let us look at the problems each family member has to face at the present time.

Mr. Smith. Mr. Smith has a work problem and this will not be solved by the employment exchange giving him the addresses of vacancies. He has a financial problem too. As an unskilled and rather unreliable man, he may earn, say, £10 5s. per week.* From the point of view of housekeeping, this income is uncertain owing to Mr. Smith's frequent change of job. Jean may earn £3 15s. per week and give her mother sometimes as much as £3, but she is also often out of work and then, being under 16, cannot apply in her own right for national assistance or for unemployment benefit (too few stamps on her card). The one constant figure is the family allowance, payable to Mrs. Smith, and totalling £1 18s. (None for the eldest child still at school, 8s. for Arthur, 10s. for each of the younger ones.) At its best, therefore, the family income will be £15 3s., but it is erratic. On national assistance, with Jean out of work, the family would have a total income of £14 12s. 6d.

The rent might be 42s. For the year 1964–5 the Institute of Municipal Treasurers and Accountants showed that a three-bedroomed council house might command rents varying between 9s. 9d. per week and £6 19s. Many areas operate rent rebate schemes whereby it is possible for a rent as high as £2 5s. to be

* These figures, and others in this chapter, are related to probabilities in 1965.

reduced to nothing. Let us assume that there is no rent rebate scheme for the district in which the Smiths live and put the rent about half way along the scale of possibilities.

Out of this income, less the rent, the family must cover, for two adults and six children, food, fuel and light, household replacements and cleaning materials, clothing and repairs. In addition, there are the personal needs of the family members. Mr. Smith has fares to work and drinks. Mrs. Smith never goes out but she watches television and smokes. The children should need money for clubs and outings, books and toys. The family should sometimes go out together or have a holiday. But budgeting on their income would be difficult for an intelligent, well-educated and sensible person—it is quite beyond Mrs. Smith. As Mr. Smith works intermittently and his income fluctuates, he has become accustomed to living from one day to the next without planning ahead. The family do not go short of food or essential clothing, but the rent arrears mount up and Mr. Smith has received an eviction notice. This makes him feel desperate and Mrs. Smith nags him—so he spends longer in the pub. (In fact, such a large family is not likely to be evicted from council property, but notices to quit are often sent to families who are in arrears with their rent in the hope that this will impel them to pay up. There is now a growing tendency to refer such families to the children's department for appropriate help, and many schemes have been started to guarantee the rent while the family is in difficulties.)

Mrs. Smith. Mrs. Smith has been married to Mr. Smith for a long time, but he used not to be so bad tempered. She has given up trying to budget and organize the home as the task seems hopelessly beyond her, so she buys food from hand to mouth and lets the rest look after itself. Also she is physically and emotionally tired of having babies and does not welcome her husband's sexual advances. But Mr. Smith is proud of his family—it makes him feel a man. There is a marital problem, brought to a head by the last pregnancy; Mrs. Smith is depressed and ill and fears she will harm the baby.

Of course, all these stresses and strains reflect on the children, but they have their individual problems too.

Jean (15). Left school last term, stays out late and has changed jobs twice already. Helps with the baby. She knows a good deal about sex from her friends, but what has she learned about marriage?

George (12). Rather delicate as a baby and has always been mother's favourite. Since his transfer to secondary school has consistently failed to attend.

Arthur (10). At a school for educationally subnormal children. Making good progress.

Peter (9). Attends junior school. Enjoys it but is mischievous. Father's favourite.

Timmy (4). Uncontrolled, demanding child. Gets told off by everyone, which makes him worse.

Mary (4 weeks). Underweight. Source of anxiety due to mother's apathetic and rejecting attitudes.

Every single member of this family, with the possible exception of Peter, has a problem which he or she has not succeeded in solving from his or her own resources. Let us now look at the way the individual members think and feel about each other.

Mr. Smith is very fond of his children, but he is not a very successful father. He makes a favourite of Peter and "picks on" Timmy; he ignores the baby and has a rather uneasy relationship with Jean. He does not have much to do with George and Arthur.

Mrs. Smith loves her children and does not like them to be away from home. George has always been her favourite, but she and Jean are also very close to each other. Timmy gets on her nerves and she is upset at not loving the baby. Jean is a "little mother" to the others, particularly the baby. The four boys play well together.

Let us now consider how this family links up with the existing social work services. Most families are usually able to manage their own problems or, if they are in trouble, are intelligent and self-confident enough to obtain what they need. From research,[1] there is some evidence that the people best served by the health and education services are middle-class people who are confident enough to demand what they want and to complain when it is not forthcoming, i.e. the social services often serve best those people who are best able to manage their affairs for themselves, and, in this sense, *need* the services least. The Smiths are not middle class or self-confident, and the following services are available to them.

MR. SMITH

> *Work problem:* employment exchanges (including disablement resettlement officers and centres for rehabilitation).
>
> *Income maintenance:* unemployment benefit (if eligible); national assistance (now administered by the Ministry of Social Security).
>
> *Rent arrears:* housing officials of local authority.
>
> *Marital problem:* probation officer; marriage guidance counsellor.

MRS. SMITH

> *Health problems:*
>
>> *Physical:* general practitioner and hospital services (including medical social worker).
>>
>> *Mental:* general practitioner; mental welfare officer; and mental hospital (including psychiatric social worker).
>>
>> *Child care problems:* home help service; health visitor; child care officer; N.S.P.C.C.; and family planning.

JEAN

> *Possibly beyond control and falling into moral danger:* probation officer; moral welfare worker; and child care officer.
>
> *Work problem:* youth employment officer.

GEORGE

> *Persistent non-attender at school:* education welfare officer; child guidance clinic; and child care officer.

ARTHUR

   Educationally subnormal: visitor from education department
      (special services section).

The following agencies would be available in a few areas only:
   Family casework section of the local authority health committee.
   Council of social service—personal service section.
   Family service unit.
In London the children's care committees and the Family Welfare
   Association would be available.

It is clear that if the Smiths had been self-confident, well-
educated and intelligent, most of their needs could be met by
these services. But they are suspicious, ill-educated and probably
unintelligent and such a complex network of services would
appear to be an inappropriate way of meeting their needs.
Furthermore, although the available services *could* help with most
problems, there are evident gaps. For example, Mrs. Smith has
never mastered the basic skills of home-making and budgeting—
who can teach her? This is too time-consuming for the health
visitor to undertake. A home help would do the work *for* her, but
few local authorities provide home helps who are trained to *teach*
rather than *act*. Timmy's development is in some danger as he
appears to be used as the family scapegoat and blamed for everything. As a result, he is becoming a demanding and difficult child,
and thus evokes more blame. But he may be too young for the
child guidance clinic which tends only to accept children of
school age.

   In brief, a service is available to meet most needs, but, on this
basis, the family may have to co-operate with about a dozen
people—not an easy task at all, and in several instances there are
alternative people who could perform the same function—for
example, either the probation officer or the marriage guidance
counsellor could offer marital counselling. How does the client
know which is the "best buy"?

Let us now leave this "service-centred" approach on one side and try to focus in a different way on this family and its needs.

In some of these problems the school is closely involved, so let us look more closely at George, aged 12. George is a persistent absentee from school. The education welfare officer has checked up and found that he has not been ill. He has questioned him about school, but cannot find anything he does not like. He has urged the parents to make sure he goes and pointed out that they could be prosecuted. After this George was absent more than ever, but did not always go home. On one occasion he stole 2s. 6d. from a sweet shop counter. In this way the probation officer became involved, but the case could also have been referred to the child care officer ("preventing delinquency") or to the child guidance clinic ("disturbed behaviour—school refusal").

George has not been at the secondary school for long; before that he attended a junior school near his home, where his attendance was fairly regular. He is a docile lad, but does not mix much with other boys, and never approaches the teacher of his own free will. His work is average but deteriorating, and, when questioned, he says that school is "all right". The teacher is friendly and helpful but feels he is getting a politely negative response. George does not seem to be bullied; he does not seem to dislike particularly any lesson or games period, although his attention is apt to wander. He has not been punished. There are not many clues to help the teacher—but there are some. Remoteness, not mixing with the other boys, day-dreaming, deteriorating work—George has never really joined in as a member of the school community. He "belongs" somewhere else. In this case it looks as if he was rejecting the school less because of bad or frightening aspects of school life* than because his thoughts are drawn somewhere else.

It is less difficult for the social worker to follow these clues as for him the picture of the family as a whole will gradually unfold—

---

* A new secondary school often *is* very frightening and this is probably a contributory factor. See Kahn and Nursten, *Unwillingly to School*, Pergamon Press, 1964.

a picture of worried and unhappy people. There is a very close bond between George and his mother (he was a delicate baby and the eldest son) and now his mother is ill, unhappy and harassed by debts—of course George is worried. The situation is not particularly new, but when George was at the primary school he was very near and could nip home at dinner time to make sure his mother was all right. Now he is too far away and a whole day is a long time to worry.

In addition, George takes his mother's side against his father— he had learned from his mother to see his father as overbearing and yet inept as a breadwinner. His father feels a failure in his son's eyes and reasserts his position by punishing. So George sees adult men as domineering and punishing and steers clear of his man teacher. (He had mainly women teachers at his junior school.)

The money-stealing episode still needs to be accounted for. On that day, George had gone to school and retreated towards home— but he knew that his mother would tell him off, particularly since the education welfare officer's visit. So there he was—he could not go back to school and he could not go home—and it was dinner time. . . .

So the pieces begin to fall into place, and certain points emerge quite clearly.

(1) This is a family problem—it is no use treating George by himself.

(2) The family problems are complex and numerous—a teacher has neither the time nor the professional equipment to tackle them all.

(3) George's problems are school-centred. Treatment must therefore proceed on two fronts, school and home, and the teacher's participation is vital.

There is no one "correct" way of tackling such a complex situation, but it is perhaps helpful to think out one possible approach to treatment, in an attempt to clarify the respective roles of school and social work agency.

The social worker would, to a certain extent, find that the pattern of her work was dictated by the immediacy of the respective problems. For example, Mrs. Smith's depression and the linked problem of the baby's health will probably need her most urgent attention, in collaboration with the health visitor and the general practitioner, who will call on such hospital facilities as may be needed. Once Mrs. Smith and the baby are "out of danger", whether this be due to casework help and support or medical treatment or a combination of both, George will feel less worried and Mrs. Smith may feel more able to look at and talk about her relationships with her other children. As she begins to realize that the social worker cares about *her* and *her* problems, accepting without criticizing, her unconscious urge to use her own children to fulfil her own emotional needs may lessen, enabling her to allow George more opportunity to lead his own separate life, without expecting constant reassurance of his "caring" (shown by worrying about her).

As the relationship of trust and confidence grows between the social worker and the family members, Mr. Smith may be encouraged to feel more confident in communicating with George and helped to see how the boy needs from him a role model of manly behaviour. Mr. Smith does not feel very successful as a man, anyway, but he and George can probably help each other if they can be helped to begin somewhere—perhaps with a shared activity as a starting point.

From the presenting problems of illness and truancy (not forgetting Jean and her problems), the social worker may gradually move towards the central problem of the parents' relationship to each other—listening, as they remember how the present grew out of the past, and helping them to have the confidence and perseverance to look at what they are doing to each other and to have hope for the future.

Ideally, Mr. Smith would find for himself ways of operating as breadwinner, as husband and as father, which he could accept as consonant with his self-respect and yet which were not beyond

F

his capacity to manage. Equally Mrs. Smith, feeling better in health and given more realistic support by her husband and children, might find it easier to allow the members of her family to be themselves, without burdening them with dependent clinging or random blaming. But perfect solutions never happen, and success is always partial.

Even if the personal relationships in this family improve following the intervention of a social caseworker, the worker's role is not limited to this particular function. Improved self-esteem may improve Mr. Smith's capacity for retaining a job, but will not alter the low wages he earns or lower his rent. According to Abel-Smith and Townsend,[2] over a third of all poor people were in a household headed by a man in full-time work, and in 1960 there were $2\frac{1}{4}$ million children in poorer households. The immediate causes of poverty are mainly old age and large families. (In this study the level of living of National Assistance Board applicants was taken as a measure of the lowest level of living regarded as acceptable by society.) Poverty is a matter for legislation based on evidence which the social worker is well-placed to provide, and for local government action, such as rent rebate schemes, which are also directly the concern of the social worker. Social casework and social action are indivisible.

Let us move our focus now back to George at school. It is the role of the social worker to explain to the school (with the family's agreement) the pattern of interaction which lies behind George's "problem" behaviour. Together the teacher and social worker must work out how the school will co-operate in the treatment plan.

For George, the male teacher has a vital role to play. George has learned that adult men in positions of authority are hostile and punishing and therefore to be avoided. This attitude needs to be replaced by the attitude that people in authority can usually be expected to be fair, reasonable and helpful, and of course George needs to learn how to approach such people in order to elicit a favourable response of this kind (i.e. not by avoidance).

His social skills *vis-à-vis* the peer group are probably also distorted, and he may need help to become an accepted and confident member of the group. His ability to learn in class does not yet seem to be seriously impaired, but needs watching as he has probably dropped behind owing to absence and he may either give up the struggle to catch up or build haphazardly on shaky foundations.

For George and his family this is a moment of crisis. Intensive help at this time can prevent formidable consequences. In the case of George himself, once a pattern of regular attendance at the secondary school, together with full participation in the school community and the enjoyment of reasonable success, can be established, he is likely to move steadily forwards. If the present school–home deadlock cannot be broken, the future is bleak indeed. For his family the help of many "experts", teachers, social workers, health experts and administrators is needed, but unless one person can hold the threads and gain the confidence of the family as a whole, piecemeal solutions will inhibit rather than help the movement towards reconciliation and independence within the family.

THE PROCESS

Perhaps at this point it may be appropriate to attempt to describe professional social work. The trained social caseworker from any setting will approach the problem in three stages (which overlap with each other in time).

(1) He will study the problem, systematically collecting information.

(2) He will try to fit the pieces of information together in order to build his first hypothesis, the tentative answer to the question "What is the matter?"

(3) He will decide what action is needed and carry out this treatment plan, modifying it as further information becomes available.

Treatment may take many forms but is based on the assumption that the family (or individual) needs a mediator between themselves and their environment, or help in understanding and modifying their own behaviour or both together. Many elements may be combined in this task, for example:

(a) Meeting straightforward material needs, e.g. shoes, or giving information, e.g. "You are entitled to free dinners".

(b) Explanations: "If you do this the following consequences will ensue because . . . ." (Easily slips into exhortation and rebuke!)

(c) Filling up the gaps in social learning, e.g. teaching Mrs. Smith to cook and budget.

(d) Supportive casework. Founded on a reliable, accepting professional relationship, listening and encouraging, being there in spite of hostility and stress, so that the client feels it is safe to try something new, because the social worker will not leave him in the lurch. Often this relationship has in it elements of the "good parent" that the client never knew, providing protection which enables the delayed process of maturation to go forward.

(e) Setting limits—the professional use of authority. Again there are elements of the "good parent" who sets clear boundaries—"because I care about you I will not let you harm yourself or damage others".

(f) Achieving understanding. Our patterns of behaviour evolve over time as the best way we can find of managing in our particular environment. Often the first "coping response" is very inefficient but is perpetuated because we have not the confidence and initiative to try something different. Families in need of social work help show much maladaptive behaviour and sometimes they are intelligent enough, and feel safe enough, to see for themselves what has happened and even to break the long-established habits of past behaviour. For example, Mr. Smith might be able to admit to himself that he felt rejected and devalued by everyone—family of origin, his own wife and children, his workmates—all except his drinking companions whose love could be bought. He could probably only begin to look at such painful things if he had begun to feel that his wife and children really needed him and that the social worker would accept him in spite of all his inadequacies.

Family troubles are a very vicious circle. As pressures increase, anxiety increases, too, and coping responses become more random and less efficient. People may be under stress "by their own fault", because they are stupid or aggressive or inefficient, but adding to the stress certainly in many cases lessens their chances of successfully solving their problems. (This was the effect of the eviction notice on the Smiths and also of the education welfare officer's visit.)

Thus social work is a disciplined activity, aiming to support the fundamental pattern of the family in such a way that each individual member's "emotional supplies" are safeguarded. At the same time, in those areas of functioning where such help is needed, the social worker will interpret the family's needs to other professional workers (schools, doctors, etc.) and to the community as a whole. This does not imply any infringement of the family's privacy, but help to families in need cannot ignore community attitudes. A family in need evokes either a helpful response or indignant cries of "they ought to be put away", i.e. they deserve to be punished and we do not want them here. It is part of the social worker's role to promote mutual understanding so that troubles of any kind may be faced and tackled and not "swept under the carpet" and hidden from sight. All social workers know of the tremendous fund of eager kindness available in any community, but we have not yet learned how to make sure it does not run to waste.

TRAINING FOR THE TASK

If professional social work is a disciplined and orderly activity, it follows that there must be a body of knowledge and skills which can be identified, taught and applied, and that the client has a right to expect a professional service from workers whose recognized training is a guarantee of basic competence. Like teaching, social work is a graduate and non-graduate profession, but still contains a large number of untrained personnel in some branches. Conditions of entry to training for the various services are complicated and constantly changing, but certain broad generalizations may be made.[3]

1. For People with a University Entrance Qualification

    (a) University course leading to a social science qualification, followed by a 1-year applied social studies course either at a university or at the Institute of Medical Social Work or at Rainer House (for probation officers).

    (b) For people who hold a degree in subjects outside the social sciences there are special university courses which combine the teaching of social science and social work.

    (c) Four-year courses at first degree level, combining social science and social work.

2. For People without a University Entrance Qualification

A variety of courses are available in technical colleges, in university extra-mural departments and at the National Institute of Social Work Training. The 2-year courses leading to the national Certificate in Social Work provide a basic generic training. The 2-year child care courses cater for people over 25 who wish to enter the child care field. There is also a 1-year probation course for men and women over 27 and several 1-year courses for experienced people in other fields.

It is not easy to summarize the central core of social work training in a few phrases, but it is perhaps possible to construct a grossly over-simplified model.

A social worker faces two ways—he must understand and use the forces moving towards social reform (as many personal needs are due to impersonal factors such as market forces), and he must understand and be able to use such knowledge as is available concerning the developmental processes of human life. Thus the social worker will learn about administration and policy—how ideas develop and grow and are translated into administrative processes. He will learn to identify the structure of society, to understand population changes and the growth and change of social institutions—in all this he will be dealing with trends and total figures. Simultaneously, he will learn to look at even the smallest parts of human behaviour as carefully and objectively as possible—he will try to disentangle why this baby responds to his mother in this particular way, why this particular child is always the "bad boy" in the family, why this father is a "good chap" in the pub but an outcast at work, why this particular community is so intolerant of the eccentric behaviour of the mentally ill. At the same time the professional social worker will learn to analyse and evaluate his own part in helping to resolve the problem of his clients. Is he, by giving, casting himself in the role of indulgent mother (a gratifying role too!) so that the client becomes the protected, dependent child? Or is he, like a good parent, creating for the client a "safe place", with pressures held at bay, where it is not too dangerous to try out new coping responses? Is he really helping the client to understand things for himself or is he really telling him what is right (another tempting role!)? Finally, the social worker must build in to his work a constant process of asking—Why did I do this? Was it useful? Would something different be better?

The first and most highly developed social work skill, taught on all recognized courses, is social casework—the ability to use a professional relationship to help a client gain confidence and understanding so that he can move of his own accord towards a solution of his problems. To this basic skill has been added the ability to work with families where the needs of each individual complement or conflict with the needs of the other family members. Here the process is similar—to help the family to understand itself; to talk out, rather than act out, its difficulties. From this a further step for some students is to work with individuals in a group, where the processes in the group itself are harnessed to help the individual members. It is easy to imagine that for some people a group ("we're all in the same boat") is less threatening than a one-to-one relationship with someone who looks like a powerful authority. Finally, professional social work, born in the clinical setting of child guidance clinics and mental hospitals, is moving further and further into the community field and here, it would seem, lies the principal challenge of the future.

THE WAY AHEAD

Until quite recently social needs, like many physical ones, were identified (diagnosed) and some treatment specific to the need was devised in the belief that, if services were provided to meet every need, people would make rational use of what was provided for them. Only today are we beginning to unravel the complicated problem of why the services meet the needs of some people and not others.

It has been said that Freud "disturbed the sleep of the world" and certainly Freud was the arch-destroyer of the myth of the rational man driven by self-interest. We have now far more knowledge of the instinctual drives, the unconscious and distorted motivations, the feelings carried over from the past, which influence human behaviour. At the same time sociologists have shown how "no man is an island", but each of us is shaped and held fast by the social pressures and patterns of the network of people and groups in which we live. We now realize that it is not enough for a service to be there—the people who need it most may

be least able to use it. Many old people feel that it is degrading
to ask for national assistance (the Poor Law deterrent is still alive
for them); others may despair before they can begin to ask for
help. For example, a man who sees himself as a failure will do
nothing rather than risk another rebuff, or some people may be
afraid because of their inner uncertainties—fears of "what the
neighbours think", fears of what the powerful officials ("they")
will say or do. Grown-up people and disturbed or delinquent
children show the same irrational behaviour patterns, "freezing"
under stress, or hitting out wildly or running away. The new
element in social work since the thirties is a growing endeavour
to make systematic use of the insights provided by psychology or
sociology both as a means towards understanding and helping the
users of the social services and as guidelines in shaping more
effective and dynamic administrative processes.

As the social services were developing, appropriate institutions
were built to which the "patients" could be admitted. This had
a dual function for the community:

(a) Something was seen to be being done to deal with the
    "sick" (cure or reform or care) so the community need not
    feel guilty about them.
(b) The "sick" were isolated from the community and therefore
    the community could feel safe.

This principle can be seen to have operated for many groups—
the mentally ill, criminals, old people, deprived children, etc.
(being "put away"). It is only fairly recently that the results
achieved by these means have been widely questioned and the
feedback is disturbing. This was easiest to see in the case of insti-
tutionalized deprived children, whose capacity for making human
relationships was permanently impaired,[4] but the same process
in varying degrees has now been recognized in hospitals, prisons,
approved schools, old people's homes and mental hospitals. The
new questions are interesting ones. Why spend so much money
on costly staff and buildings which often seem to hinder rather

than help the "patient's" recovery? How can we work with the "patient" and the community so that he can live successfully in the place where he belongs? We still lack the services, personnel and technical skill to carry out these new ideas, but this is the direction in which we are moving fast, possibly indeed running before we can walk. The Mental Health Act, 1959 (coinciding with modern methods of treatment), changed the mental hospital's role from that of asylum for the many to asylum (in the original sense of "safe refuge") for the few and treatment centre for the many, with the onus laid on the mental welfare officer to work with the patient and his family in the community. The Children and Young Persons Act, 1963, laid on children's departments the duty of preventing children from coming into care and of preventing delinquency, i.e. helping families in the community before they begin to break up. Hardly had this Act become law before the Kilbrandon Report in Scotland and the Labour Party's report, *Crime, a Challenge to us All*, had suggested a new kind of service to replace the present arrangements, and then, in August 1965, the Government White Paper, *The Child, the Family and the Young Offender* (Cmnd. 2742), put forward even more far-reaching proposals designed to help the child and his family in cases of difficulty or delinquency. The White Paper stated the Government's belief that the various services connected with the support of the family "should be organized as a family service", but did not attempt to set out any blueprint for this fundamental reorganization. It proposed that all children under 16 (the proposed school leaving age) who had committed an offence, or failed to attend school or were believed to be in need of help because of lack of care or discipline in the home, should be dealt with by family councils instead of the present juvenile courts. In the relatively infrequent cases where the facts are in dispute the case would be referred to a family court.

More recently (October 1966) a Scottish White Paper *Social Work and the Community* (Cmnd. 3065) was published. It proposed the establishment of a unified local authority social work department covering all aspects of social welfare, including probation, and the use of childrens panels to replace juvenile courts. This seems to herald the end of the social services as the Smith family experienced them.

In these chapters social workers have appeared under their departments as organized in 1965, but the case material demonstrates what the most recent White Papers have argued—that there is considerable overlap of function between the present services, so that either the probation officer, or the child care officer, or the psychiatric social worker (or several voluntary organizations), might have become responsible for the same family and, as professional social workers, their method of working would have differed little, except on account of the limitations of their agency. For example, neither the probation officer nor the psychiatric social worker is empowered by law to give help in kind or in cash—but the child care officer has these powers. Neither the child care officer nor the probation officer is likely to have easy access to psychiatric consultation; this is more readily available to the psychiatric social worker. These differences are more like restrictive practices than true divisions of function.

So the objectives of social work never stand still. At first social workers were concerned to help people whose lives were damaged to rehabilitate themselves; now the focus has shifted to trying to prevent the damage by intervening at the earliest possible warning signal. Another shift in focus can be seen as a logical consequence—that the social services should see themselves as geared to the promotion of positive mental health—a vast aim which would draw in the combined efforts of teachers, doctors, nurses, social workers and many people in the community as well, and would imply a far more methodical use of the knowledge we already hold as well as the development of better technical skills and further understanding of human relations.

REFERENCES

1. Political and Economic Planning, *Family Needs and the Social Services*, Allen & Unwin, 1961.
   Douglas, J. W. B., *The Home and the School*, McGibbon & Kee, 1964.
2. Abel-Smith, B. and Townsend, P., *The Poor and the Poorest*, Bell, 1965.
3. Further details of training facilities are contained in the following publications: *Training and Employment in Social Work*, prepared by the Women's Employment Federation and the Information Department of the National Council for Social Service, 1964 (price 5s.), new edition planned for 1966; *Education for Social Work in the Universities*, Joint University Council for Social and Public Administration (pamphlet); *The Social Workers*, B.B.C. publication, 1965 (price 8s. 6d.); *Women and Work*, B.B.C. publication, 1965 (price 6s.).
4. Bowlby, J., *Child Care and the Growth of Love*, Pelican, 1965 ed.

APPENDICES

SOCIETY is not static; it is constantly changing, and with it the individual needs of its members. To meet these needs new organizations spring up, and just as the organization and content of education are always changing, so does the voluntary sector of social work reach out to help those who are in special need at particular points of time. In the following three appendices brief accounts are given of the formation, growth and functions of three organizations, all quite different in purpose, constitution and in the rate of their development; they were not chosen because they have anything in common other than that they illustrate the process whereby social service meets social need quickly and in a practical fashion. They could be matched by many other similar bodies, but all of them have close links with education, and all demonstrate the essential point that the educational system can no longer exist in splendid isolation from the environment in which it works.

THE YOUNG PEOPLE'S
CONSULTATION CENTRE

HILARY HALPIN, J.P.

Liaison Officer to the Hampstead Centre

THE objects of the Young People's Consultation Centre, set up in Hampstead by the Youth Studies and Research Foundation in June 1961, were threefold.

(1) To provide a walk-in Centre where young people between the ages of 14 and 25 with any sort of problem could come and get free, confidential advice from highly skilled professional workers.

(2) To do research into the kind of problems which were brought to the Centre and to evolve techniques for interviewing adolescents.

(3) To provide the opportunity for a free exchange of knowledge with other workers in the field by means of seminars, study groups, etc.

The Centre was originally started in two rooms in Burgh House, Hampstead, a free-standing Queen Anne Mansion in its own garden, belonging to the Hampstead Borough Council. For the purpose of a young people's consultation centre there were two main assets, firstly, that the Council of Social Service in the basement office was prepared to answer the telephone and book appointments, thus eliminating the need for full-time office staff at the beginning, and, secondly, there was a certain anonymity for youngsters since many other activities took place at Burgh House. These other meetings could, however, create confusion and when in 1964 the Centre moved to a converted shop with rooms above in a quiet street, it was felt that despite the camouflage provided at Burgh House, the new premises at 11 King's College Road were infinitely more satisfactory. The present accommodation provides a ground floor office and waiting room, with four consulting rooms upstairs, and a small room on the ground floor can be used as an extra office or consulting room as necessary.

The three officers of the Youth Studies and Research Foundation decided from the beginning that the Centre should be psychoanalytically orientated, and with this in mind appointed a staff of four, in the first place, and later six analysts and psychotherapists. This psychoanalytical slant did not presuppose that all the queries and problems would be psychoanalytical and the Centre was prepared to arrange for legal advice, to help with careers, and to provide information about clubs and hostels or to meet any other need. Publicity for the Centre was aimed at adolescents direct and also at those people in the community likely to refer adolescents to the Centre. A folder and a poster were designed giving the address, the days and times of interviews, and a statement that all discussions were confidential. These posters were sent to public libraries, youth employment offices, schools, art schools and colleges of further education; the small folder was left in coffee bars and other likely places.

The adults who might refer adolescents were invited to coffee parties in order that they might meet the consultants and reassure themselves about the kind of service offered. It was interesting that although one coffee party was held in a November fog and another on the evening of a bus strike, almost everyone came who had been invited.

As press publicity was built up requests came from all over the British Isles from individuals and organizations interested in starting something similar. The six consultants are available at the Centre three nights a week from 6 p.m. to 10 p.m. and on Saturday mornings. All the consultants work during the day with young people or children and the principle has been established that no one shall be asked to work more than two evenings, or one evening and Saturday morning, averaging approximately 7 hours a week each. Of this, $5\frac{1}{2}$ hours is used for seeing clients and the remaining time taken up with recording and staff discussion. Each interview lasts about 50 minutes. At the beginning youngsters could walk in and be seen within the hour, but more recently most appointments are made by telephone or by letter. However, if anyone should walk in and is prepared to wait, one of the consultants will always see them for 10 minutes or so between appointments, to satisfy themselves that the youngster is not at risk and to make another appointment. It has been found at times, generally in response to magazine or newspaper publicity, that the waiting list has grown too long and when this happens and clients are asked to wait more than a week or 10 days, the appointments fail to be kept. The adolescent's problems are urgent today, and they cannot wait until tomorrow. Also in response to publicity a number of letters have come in from all over England setting out the individual's problem in great detail, where possible and in order to save the expense of several visits to London these correspondents are referred to someone reliable in their locality.

As well as six consultants there are two secretary-receptionists and a psychiatric social worker for one and a half sessions a week. A general practitioner, a psychiatrist and a clinical psychologist are available for consultation if needed.

Any young person coming to the Centre is asked only for his name and address and whether he would prefer to see a man or a woman. There is no form-filling and most of the information about the clients is gathered by the consultants during the interview and recorded afterwards. Since 1 June 1961 over 600 clients have been seen and over 2400 interviews have been given. The age range is officially from 14 to 25, but there is no rigid rule and people have been seen in the 12 to 30 age range. The most frequent age group seen has been from 17 to 19. They come from all over London, the Home Counties, and a few from places further afield such as the Midlands, Scotland and the Republic of Ireland. About half of them are referred by social workers, doctors, youth leaders, schools and further education colleges. The remainder refer themselves or are recommended by satisfied clients. A small number have appointments made for them by parents, relatives or parents' friends. Occasionally, an au pair girl or an immigrant will be advised to come by an almost total stranger who has heard of the Centre. A small number of parents have come without their children, usually seeking advice or support. The numbers of boys and girls are roughly equal and they come from all five social groups—from the youngster with an intelligence quotient of 70 to the graduate.

The problems range from those that can be dealt with in one or two interviews (where can one make up a deficiency of appropriate O- or A-levels in order to follow a specific course? What is the legal position of a couple of 17 wishing to get married?) to the more complex problems of interpersonal relationships. Most adolescents get through adolescence with the help of their own age group; the ones who come to the Centre bring problems they feel unable to discuss with their peers, such as feelings of inadequacy, fear of homosexuality, and amongst the girls an inability to make friends and personality difficulties.

The consultant has to assess fairly quickly whether it is sufficient to deal with the problem as it is presented to him or whether the adolescent's need is such that it will take several interviews before he acknowledges the underlying difficulty and before it is possible for him to accept this as part of a movement toward maturity.

A certain number of young people, while not being deeply disturbed, need help over a longer period than the Centre can afford to give without creating a bottleneck; these, in consultation with the psychiatrist, are referred elsewhere for treatment.

It is proposed during 1966 to do intensive research on the 600 or so files at the Centre with a view to evaluating the work done and to answering the following four broad questions of basic interest to all who work with young people.

(a) Who were they?
(b) Why did they come?
(c) What was found out about them?
(d) What happened to them?

Owing to the strict confidentiality of the work there has never been any follow-up at the Centre, with the exception of those cases put into treatment when the therapists concerned provide 2-monthly reports, and this group, about which there is much more information available, may prove invaluable.

The educational activities at the Centre have been mainly concerned with running seminars for social workers. Two of these run in 1965 were heavily over-subscribed, which indicates the dearth of this kind of seminar in the community. Papers were read about the work of the Centre and cases were presented for discussion. The Centre staff certainly derived great help from meeting and talking with other people whose work is with adolescents. Study evenings for specific groups such as juvenile court magistrates, child care officers, and so on, have been run, and consultants have also been asked to spend two or three sessions in a children's department running a discussion group. There have been also a number of parties of students, health visitors and others who have come for a morning or an afternoon. It is difficult in many instances to distinguish between what might be classed as publicity and what might formally be called education, but nearly always there is a two-way sharing of information.

The Centre has felt that one of i's important functions was to record information about other centres being started, to put people in touch with each other in order to avoid overlap, and to give any possible help they can and to those who are engaged in similar work. The main difficulties have been firstly financial, and, secondly, a shortage of skilled personnel. Nearly all the organizations have been obliged to use competent lay staff for the preliminary interviews, to employ a panel of lay and professional staff on a rota, or to resort to the anonymity of a telephone advice service which then puts the client in touch with an expert if necessary. No centre has quite the same pattern; each one has simply found that there is a need to be met, and has set out to provide it.

The following is a list of those centres which are actually running, but about another twenty are in the process of being set up.

Manchester: Young People's Advice Centre, 50 Bridge Street, Manchester.

Exeter: Young People's Consultation Centre, 2 Waterbeer Street, Exeter.

Edinburgh: Young People's Advisory Service, Cephas House, Edinburgh.

New Ham, London: London Borough of New Ham Health Department, 99 The Grove, Stratford, E. 15.

Bristol: Bristol Marriage and Family Guidance Council, 7 Berkeley Square, Bristol 8.

Gloucester: Young People's Advice Centre (sponsored by Gloucestershire Standing Conference on Family Life).

Liverpool: Young Persons' Advisory Service, 34 Stanley Street, Liverpool 1 (organized by Liverpool Personal Service Society).

Wolverhampton: Y.W.C.A. Central Office, Penn Road, Wolverhampton (Young People's Telephone Advisory Service).

Some of these centres may change their addresses from time to time. Information about their location will usually be available at the nearest Citizens' Advice Bureau.

CHILDREN'S HOUSE

OLIVE KENDON

IN THE winter of 1940–1, when England's war efforts were at their peak, able-bodied men and women from all walks of life were commandeered for service leaving some of the less capable and ailing people to run the ordinary chores of the country's living. Fathers were soldiering, mothers making munitions, and the teachers who remained were outnumbered to such an extent by children that, after school hours, in our large cities especially, the main bulk of our child population were roaming the streets cold, dirty, hungry and undisciplined.

Into this maelstrom I suddenly found myself wandering one Sunday morning along a large square of half-demolished back-to-back slum dwellings where the depressing sight was outmatched by raucous shouts from the throats of restless children, one of whom ran up to me shouting "Miss! Them two's fighting!" At this I intervened, and when they had quietened down one asked me "Please can we have a Sunday School?" and, as I hesitated, "Miss, when can it start?" claimed another voice.

This clarion call was not to be denied. Five adults, two men and three women, barely acquainted, met together and hired a room near at hand for two evenings a week for the purpose of keeping these children busy with their hands. Although materials were scarce children were not. In a fortnight we rented another room, and before the end of another month we obtained a large empty house-and-shop in a nearby street. Here one Sunday afternoon I stood surrounded by a group of about thirty children aged from about 3 to 13. I said: "We've found a house for our club and it's to be *your* house. IT'S NOT MINE, and you can do what you like in it. Go in carefully because the stairs are rather steep. Big ones, look after the little ones."

I put the key in the lock and opened the door. I was almost pushed to the floor with the hurricane that rushed past me with joyous shouts. I waited inside the front shop. Soon the excitement died down and they stood around me waiting.

"It's very dirty," I said, "we can't work in it like this."

"Miss, we can clean it," was the immediate response.

"Can you? But what are we going to do for brooms and buckets?"

"Bring 'em from home, Miss," they said.

"All right," I replied, "bring some soap too, if you can. I'll meet you here on Tuesday evening at six o'clock."

"Why not tomorrer?" asked one.

"Because I'm too busy at home," I replied. "Goodbye, everyone, till Tuesday."

"Tarrah, Miss", they cried as I left them to disperse.

On Tuesday evening the windows and door had been wiped as far as young arms would reach, leaving arcs of grime on the great shop panes and, when they began cleaning (with cold water in January), they discovered that the lino in the shop was a black-and-white check.

A nucleus of children continued scrubbing week after week, begging to do so also on Saturdays. Disputes sometimes arose, some of which, if not settled by one or two of the older children, were referred to the adults whose numbers were also growing.

The following letter, written by one of the older girls in reply to a child's letter appearing in the Press, will indicate how the work developed and what effect it had on the minds and hearts of the children. There is no doubt that the gift of communal responsibility in an acceptable form to pre-adolescent children by the adult world slowly rids them of their hatred of authority and sets the tone of their attitude to it for later life.

DEAR MISS LAURA,

I read with much interest your letter which was printed in the *Daily Mail* in the 5th inst.

I am fourteen years old, and I am a member of a club which is in Stockport, and it is called "Children's House". Before this club was opened I used to be like you and many other children—bored stiff trying to amuse myself when I had nothing to do—but now I can go to the club and guarantee myself that I will have a happy evening. I would like to tell you what we do at our club.

We hold our meeting in what used to be a big shop, but now it is ours. It consists of seven rooms, a bathroom and two cellars.

On Tuesday evening there is a play-hour for very young children, and woodwork class for the boys; for the girls there is a class where they sing, play games and do handcraft work, and a needlework class where we machine, sew, and do raffia work.

On Wednesdays we play games, sing, and go to our canteen for a hot supper, and to follow we have dancing, and to conclude we sing hymns.

On Thursday evenings we make puppets, read books; then we have a meeting of the club, in which we make our own rules and say what we want to do on other nights.

Friday night is the night on which we practise first aid, dance and sing hymns.

Then on Saturdays some of the children and mothers have baths; they bring a towel, soap and twopence, but when the little ones come without their mothers the girls like myself bath them. Canteen follows and then we sing and dance.

The best night of the week is Sunday. Firstly, when we go into the club we have a short service, when we sing hymns and sacred songs. This we enjoy very much. Then we go to another room where we have a helpful film. By helpful I mean a film which tells us how to understand our friends and neighbours, like David Livingstone. Or we have a lantern lecture, or a discussion group, in which we talk of various subjects. After this we go to our canteen again and refresh ourselves before we go to dancing. On Sunday evening the house is always full of children and a few mothers.

For all this enjoyment and entertainment all we pay is threepence a week, and this goes to the expenses of the club.

Well, now I have told you about our club, I suppose you wish you lived in Stockport. It would be very good if every town in England could have a club like ours, for they enjoy themselves, and also learn how to become better citizens.

I will leave you with the best wishes of the club.

Yours sincerely,

Mary . . . .

The success of this work was so cogent that when the lease of the building expired the local education authority bought it, loaning it to the Children's House and leaving it to the original committee to continue to work therein. When it was scheduled for slum clearance, the town council, rather than see the work interrupted, left the gaunt building standing amid the rubble until they had provided another building for them, the old fire station beautifully converted.

And now a town in the Midlands is planning to have a Children's House for children with a new poverty; modern, well-clad children from unsatisfactory homes, often inharmonious or broken. Commonly both parents are out at work at the end of the school day. And, even with television, of what use is a latchkey except to provide physical shelter? When parents do return home they are often too tired to bother much about their children. Thus, left out, the suffering child bottles up a feeling of resentment which, although usually hidden under a cloak of indifference, breeds hate towards the adult world of authority. The result is a breaking out eventually in some grade of delinquency. Although much is done today for adolescents the children are not noticed until they commit some crime.

To overcome this undesirable attitude towards authority the child should be helped early to co-operate with it, and this can only be achieved through his will.

It is a tremendous attraction to give children a "House" of their very own, to help to make and run. If this can be accomplished and lovingly developed then our aim is reached. This is exactly what the town in the Midlands is planning to do.

AMICI

AMICI (Friends) is an association of parents who have come together to provide counsel for people, mainly students, between the ages of about 17 and 24. Those who come to AMICI are treated as friends of the family, not as "cases", and their problems discussed in an informal but absolutely confidential manner. The basic function of the counsellors is to listen, so that the younger people can talk exhaustively, free from the emotional tensions of their own family circle. Counsellors are expected to react as experienced parents, taking a commonsense, practical view of a problem and giving constructive suggestions to help their young visitors to overcome a problem which threatens to be too much for their own unaided efforts. The member's own resources may be adequate; he may call for help on all other members; he may decide the problem needs specialist advice from people outside AMICI. He must see that his young visitors have sufficient help to avoid their being overwhelmed by difficulties and coming to be regarded as "failures". But as a prudent parent he will be concerned not to weaken anyone by giving too much help, by depriving a young person of the tonic of a successful response to a challenge. Help given in this way may not be used to prepare the way for propaganda or proselytization, nor may any fee be accepted. Members may, however, be reimbursed for heavy out-of-pocket expenses by the parents of a boy or girl assisted, if such repayment is offered.

By being "an association with a difference" AMICI is able to help young people who, for a variety of reasons, shy away from other agencies, both official and voluntary. As the association is still very small and not very widely known, since it is less than 2 years old, a member's house will often not be the first place to which a young person turns for help. It may be the last resort of the desperate. Some such have been drawn back from suicidal despair, and helped over months to re-start a successful life. But most problems are less severe and dramatic. Counsellors are none the less as "casually thorough" with the "simple" problem, recognizing that by being so they help to avert a more serious situation from developing later.

The underlying theory of AMICI is that the family is *not* a self-sufficient, viable unit, and that young people need and are entitled to find help and guidance outside their own families, such as their predecessors would have found in earlier times in the tribe, the clan and other forms of supra-familiar nexus.

By limiting membership to parents, AMICI ensures that in assisting young people the interests of their own parents and other family ties will not be forgotten. This approach is thought to be nearer to the real needs of social responsibility than the planned bureaucracy of professionalism. Members are not only parents but also busy professional people, too busy to be "busy-bodies", sympathetic but not sentimental, in good enough spiritual health to be able to help with problems without creating new ones. By helping young people to avoid failure, and by rehabilitating some who were on the verge of the last catastrophe, AMICI has added many thousands of pounds to the State and society in terms of increased earning and tax-paying capacity. This success of the "pilot scheme" justifies expansion and the full development of the ideas and ideals of AMICI in conjunction with an international philanthropic organization is being actively considered. In the meantime, all queries will be gladly answered by the Acting Secretary, 80 Hollies Avenue, West Byfleet, Surrey (Byfleet 42536).

INDEX

151